YASIR ARAFAT

MENACHEM BEGIN

TONY BLAIR

GEORGE W. BUSH

JIMMY CARTER

VICENTE FOX

SADDAM HUSSEIN

HOSNI MUBARAK

VLADIMIR PUTIN

MOHAMMED REZA PAHLAVI

ANWAR SADAT

THE SAUDI ROYAL FAMILY

Anwar
Sadat

Sara Louise Kras

CHELSEA HOUSE
PUBLISHERS
A Haights Cross Communications Company

Philadelphia

Frontispiece: Anwar Sadat was the first Egyptian president to forge a peace agreement with Israel, even though he would be forced to face the hostility of other Arab nations for his actions. He will be remembered by his people and the world for his commitment to peace.

CHELSEA HOUSE PUBLISHERS

EDITOR IN CHIEF Sally Cheney
DIRECTOR OF PRODUCTION Kim Shinners
CREATIVE MANAGER Takeshi Takahashi
MANUFACTURING MANAGER Diann Grasse

Staff for ANWAR SADAT

EDITOR Lee Marcott
ASSOCIATE EDITOR Bill Conn
PRODUCTION ASSISTANT Jaimie Winkler
PICTURE RESEARCH 21st Century Publishing and Communications, Inc.
SERIES AND COVER DESIGNER Takeshi Takahashi
LAYOUT 21st Century Publishing and Communications, Inc.

A Haights Cross Communications ✦ Company

http://www.chelseahouse.com

First Printing

1 3 5 7 9 8 6 4 2

Library of Congress Cataloging-in-Publication Data

Kras, Sara Louise.
    Anwar Sadat / Sara Louise Kras.
        v. cm.—(Major world leaders)
Includes bibliographical references and index. Contents: A hero is born—The free officers' organization—The revolution—President Gamal Abdel Nasser—Sadat takes charge—The hero of October—Journey of peace—Camp David—Assassination—Sadat's legacy.
    ISBN 0-7910-6949-4
    1. Sadat, Anwar, 1918–   —Biography—Juvenile literature. 2. Presidents—Egypt—Biography—Juvenile literature. [1. Sadat, Anwar, 1918–   . 2. Presidents—Egypt.]
I. Title. II. Series.
DT107.85 .K73 2002
962.05'4'092—dc21
                                                                2002007469

TABLE OF CONTENTS

On Leadership

Arthur M. Schlesinger, jr.

Leadership, it may be said, is really what makes the world go round. Love no doubt smoothes the passage; but love is a private transaction between consenting adults. Leadership is a public transaction with history. The idea of leadership affirms the capacity of individuals to move, inspire, and mobilize masses of people so that they act together in pursuit of an end. Sometimes leadership serves good purposes, sometimes bad; but whether the end is benign or evil, great leaders are those men and women who leave their personal stamp on history.

Now, the very concept of leadership implies the proposition that individuals can make a difference. This proposition has never been universally accepted. From classical times to the present day, eminent thinkers have regarded individuals as no more than the agents and pawns of larger forces, whether the gods and goddesses of the ancient world or, in the modern era, race, class, nation, the dialectic, the will of the people, the spirit of the times, history itself. Against such forces, the individual dwindles into insignificance.

So contends the thesis of historical determinism. Tolstoy's great novel *War and Peace* offers a famous statement of the case. Why, Tolstoy asked, did millions of men in the Napoleonic Wars, denying their human feelings and their common sense, move back and forth across Europe slaughtering their fellows? "The war," Tolstoy answered, "was bound to happen simply because it was bound to happen." All prior history determined it. As for leaders, they, Tolstoy said, "are but the labels that serve to give a name to an end and, like labels, they have the least possible connection with the event." The greater the leader, "the more conspicuous the inevitability and the predestination of every act he commits." The leader, said Tolstoy, is "the slave of history."

Determinism takes many forms. Marxism is the determinism of class. Nazism the determinism of race. But the idea of men and women as the slaves of history runs athwart the deepest human instincts. Rigid determinism abolishes the idea of human freedom—the assumption of free choice that underlies every move we make, every word we speak, every thought we think. It abolishes the idea of human responsibility, since it is manifestly unfair to reward or punish people for actions that are by definition beyond their control. No one can live consistently by any deterministic creed. The Marxist states prove this themselves by their extreme susceptibility to the cult of leadership.

More than that, history refutes the idea that individuals make no difference. In December 1931 a British politician crossing Fifth Avenue in New York City between 76th and 77th Streets around 10:30 P.M. looked in the wrong direction and was knocked down by an automobile—a moment, he later recalled, of a man aghast, a world aglare: "I do not understand why I was not broken like an eggshell or squashed like a gooseberry." Fourteen months later an American politician, sitting in an open car in Miami, Florida, was fired on by an assassin; the man beside him was hit. Those who believe that individuals make no difference to history might well ponder whether the next two decades would have been the same had Mario Constasino's car killed Winston Churchill in 1931 and Giuseppe Zangara's bullet killed Franklin Roosevelt in 1933. Suppose, in addition, that Lenin had died of typhus in Siberia in 1895 and that Hitler had been killed on the western front in 1916. What would the 20th century have looked like now?

For better or for worse, individuals do make a difference. "The notion that a people can run itself and its affairs anonymously," wrote the philosopher William James, "is now well known to be the silliest of absurdities. Mankind does nothing save through initiatives on the part of inventors, great or small, and imitation by the rest of us—these are the sole factors in human progress. Individuals of genius show the way, and set the patterns, which common people then adopt and follow."

Leadership, James suggests, means leadership in thought as well as in action. In the long run, leaders in thought may well make the greater difference to the world. "The ideas of economists and political philosophers, both when they are right and when they are wrong," wrote John Maynard Keynes, "are more powerful than is commonly understood. Indeed the world is ruled by little else. Practical men, who believe themselves to be quite exempt from any intellectual influences, are usually the slaves of some defunct economist. . . . The power of vested interests is vastly exaggerated compared with the gradual encroachment of ideas."

But, as Woodrow Wilson once said, "Those only are leaders of men, in the general eye, who lead in action.... It is at their hands that new thought gets its translation into the crude language of deeds." Leaders in thought often invent in solitude and obscurity, leaving to later generations the tasks of imitation. Leaders in action—the leaders portrayed in this series—have to be effective in their own time.

And they cannot be effective by themselves. They must act in response to the rhythms of their age. Their genius must be adapted, in a phrase from William James, "to the receptivities of the moment." Leaders are useless without followers. "There goes the mob," said the French politician, hearing a clamor in the streets. "I am their leader. I must follow them." Great leaders turn the inchoate emotions of the mob to purposes of their own. They seize on the opportunities of their time, the hopes, fears, frustrations, crises, potentialities. They succeed when events have prepared the way for them, when the community is awaiting to be aroused, when they can provide the clarifying and organizing ideas. Leadership completes the circuit between the individual and the mass and thereby alters history.

It may alter history for better or for worse. Leaders have been responsible for the most extravagant follies and most monstrous crimes that have beset suffering humanity. They have also been vital in such gains as humanity has made in individual freedom, religious and racial tolerance, social justice, and respect for human rights.

There is no sure way to tell in advance who is going to lead for good and who for evil. But a glance at the gallery of men and women in MAJOR WORLD LEADERS suggests some useful tests.

One test is this: Do leaders lead by force or by persuasion? By command or by consent? Through most of history leadership was exercised by the divine right of authority. The duty of followers was to defer and to obey. "Theirs not to reason why/Theirs but to do and die." On occasion, as with the so-called enlightened despots of the 18th century in Europe, absolutist leadership was animated by humane purposes. More often, absolutism nourished the passion for domination, land, gold, and conquest and resulted in tyranny.

The great revolution of modern times has been the revolution of equality. "Perhaps no form of government," wrote the British historian James Bryce in his study of the United States, *The American Commonwealth,* "needs great leaders so much as democracy." The idea that all people should be equal in their legal condition has undermined the old structure of authority, hierarchy, and deference. The revolution of equality has had two contrary effects on the nature of leadership. For equality, as Alexis de Tocqueville pointed out in his great study *Democracy in America*, might mean equality in servitude as well as equality in freedom.

"I know of only two methods of establishing equality in the political world," Tocqueville wrote. "Rights must be given to every citizen, or none at all to anyone . . . save one, who is the master of all." There was no middle ground "between the sovereignty of all and the absolute power of one man." In his astonishing prediction of 20th-century totalitarian dictatorship, Tocqueville explained how the revolution of equality could lead to the *Führerprinzip* and more terrible absolutism than the world had ever known.

But when rights are given to every citizen and the sovereignty of all is established, the problem of leadership takes a new form, becomes more exacting than ever before. It is easy to issue commands and enforce them by the rope and the stake, the concentration camp and the *gulag*. It is much harder to use argument and achievement to overcome opposition and win consent. The Founding Fathers of the United States understood the difficulty. They believed that history had given them the opportunity to decide, as Alexander Hamilton wrote in the first Federalist Paper, whether men are indeed capable of basing government on "reflection and choice, or whether they are forever destined to depend . . . on accident and force."

Government by reflection and choice called for a new style of leadership and a new quality of followership. It required leaders to be responsive to popular concerns, and it required followers to be active and informed participants in the process. Democracy does not eliminate emotion from politics; sometimes it fosters demagoguery; but it is confident that, as the greatest of democratic leaders put it, you cannot fool all of the people all of the time. It measures leadership by results and retires those who overreach or falter or fail.

It is true that in the long run despots are measured by results too. But they can postpone the day of judgment, sometimes indefinitely, and in the meantime they can do infinite harm. It is also true that democracy is no guarantee of virtue and intelligence in government, for the voice of the people is not necessarily the voice of God. But democracy, by assuring the right of opposition, offers built-in resistance to the evils inherent in absolutism. As the theologian Reinhold Niebuhr summed it up, "Man's capacity for justice makes democracy possible, but man's inclination to justice makes democracy necessary."

A second test for leadership is the end for which power is sought. When leaders have as their goal the supremacy of a master race or the promotion of totalitarian revolution or the acquisition and exploitation of colonies or the protection of greed and privilege or the preservation of personal power, it is likely that their leadership will do little to advance the cause of humanity. When their goal is the abolition of slavery, the liberation of women, the enlargement of opportunity for the poor and powerless, the extension of equal rights to racial minorities, the defense of the freedoms of expression and opposition, it is likely that their leadership will increase the sum of human liberty and welfare.

Leaders have done great harm to the world. They have also conferred great benefits. You will find both sorts in this series. Even "good" leaders must be regarded with a certain wariness. Leaders are not demigods; they put on their trousers one leg after another just like ordinary mortals. No leader is infallible, and every leader needs to be reminded of this at regular intervals. Irreverence irritates leaders but is their salvation. Unquestioning submission corrupts leaders and demeans followers. Making a cult of a leader is always a mistake. Fortunately hero worship generates its own antidote. "Every hero," said Emerson, "becomes a bore at last."

The signal benefit the great leaders confer is to embolden the rest of us to live according to our own best selves, to be active, insistent, and resolute in affirming our own sense of things. For great leaders attest to the reality of human freedom against the supposed inevitabilities of history. And they attest to the wisdom and power that may lie within the most unlikely of us, which is why Abraham Lincoln remains the supreme example of great leadership. A great leader, said Emerson, exhibits new possibilities to all humanity. "We feed on genius . . . . Great men exist that there may be greater men."

Great leaders, in short, justify themselves by emancipating and empowering their followers. So humanity struggles to master its destiny, remembering with Alexis de Tocqueville: "It is true that around every man a fatal circle is traced beyond which he cannot pass; but within the wide verge of that circle he is powerful and free; as it is with man, so with communities." ■

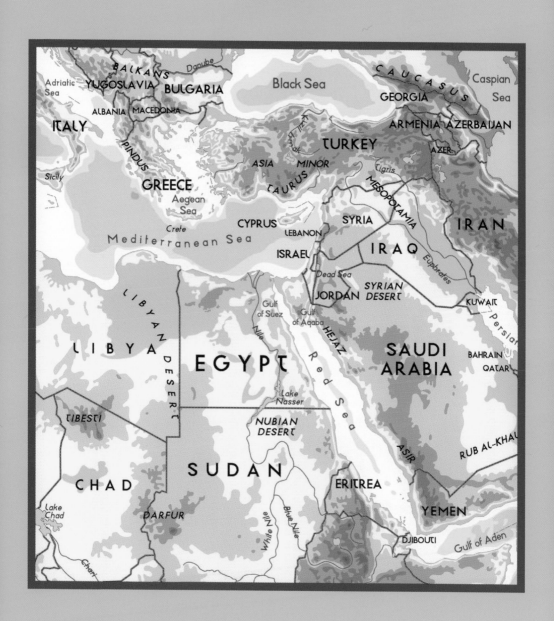

President Anwar Sadat is shown attending the military parade at which he was assassinated on October 6, 1981.

1

A Hero Is Born

On June 5, 1975, Anwar Sadat dressed in a white admiral's uniform, got into his car, and drove slowly toward the Suez Canal. Egyptians chanted Sadat's name, cheering him on as he drove toward the canal. Along the way, an old man with long white hair waved his arms desperately to stop the car. He looked serious in his white robe and leather sandals.

Guards jumped from Sadat's car to block the man. Sadat ordered them to stop. Once the man was released, he looked at Sadat for a long time and then kneeled on the paved road and started to pray. He gave a thanksgiving prayer to God. Once he finished his prayer, he stood and walked back into the crowd. This incident touched Sadat deeply, as he recalled in his autobiography, *In Search of Identity,* "That minute, short as it was, meant everything to that man. He had survived to see his homeland once again . . . he had to kneel down before God, to thank Him for sending that unexpected light to disperse the prolonged darkness he had so painfully survived."

Since 1967, Egyptians had been stripped of pride for their homeland by failed battles against the Israelis. Feelings of inferiority had run rampant among the population after the Six-Day War of 1967. Sadat's predecessor, Gamal Nasser, had led Egypt into battle against the Israelis. Not only had he lost the war, but he had also lost the precious land of the Sinai Peninsula and part of the Gaza Strip. After the Six-Day War, Israel had occupied the east side of the Suez Canal. Egypt had to close the lucrative canal for six years because of the continuing battle.

In October 1973 the Egyptians regained control of the Suez Canal and recaptured part of the Sinai Peninsula. Their leader, Anwar Sadat, had painstakingly planned a surprise battle against Israel. He was so secretive that he did not even tell all his generals. The Israelis were taken by complete surprise because they were busy observing a religious holiday, Yom Kippur. Sadat's daring came from a deep concern for Egypt's honor. In Raphael Israeli's *Man of Defiance*, Sadat is quoted as saying, "Better to die honorably than to live in humiliation."

After the battle, during negotiations with Israel, Sadat made the daring decision to reopen the Suez Canal. Because it had been closed for so long, it was littered with hundreds of thousands of land mines and bombs. Barges, boats, and oil drums had been floating in it for years. Trucks and tanks lined the bottom. The debris was removed with assistance from the United States.

On that June day in 1975, Sadat boarded the destroyer *October*. The cool air flowed across his face as he sailed through the canal that had been closed for so many years. He smiled and waved at the cheering crowd. Along the banks of the Suez Canal, banners fluttered in the wind that stated, "We Have Opened the Canal. We Will Keep it Open." Later Sadat was to recall in his autobiography, "I did all this for peace."

This flamboyant Egyptian president came from a small village at a time when Egypt was under British rule. Years later he would be instrumental in overthrowing the British government in Egypt. He served as vice president to the revolutionary leader President Gamal Nasser. Once Sadat became president, he was the first Arab leader to visit Jerusalem in hopes of making a peace agreement with Israeli Prime Minister Menachem Begin. Both Sadat and Begin were awarded the Nobel Peace Prize in 1978 in recognition of their strong desire and efforts to establish peace.

Loved by his countrymen, he was called a hero. Hated by fundamentalist Muslim countries, he was called a traitor. Although he was assassinated by his enemies, Anwar el-Sadat's legacy lives on.

Sadat was born on December 25, 1918, in a small village called Mit Abul-Kum on the Nile Delta. His humble house was made of sun-dried brick with a straw roof. Before Sadat was born, his father, Mohammed el-Sadat, and his mother, a half-Sudanese woman named Sitt-al-Barrein, lived in Sudan, where his father worked as a clerk in a military hospital for the Egyptian army.

When Sitt-al-Barrein's pregnancy advanced, she was sent back to the little village on the Nile Delta to deliver the child. Sitt-al-Barrein and Mohammed el-Sadat were the parents of three boys and one girl. Sadat had more brothers and sisters from his father's other wives. There were a total of 13 children.

His father had earned a certificate of primary education and was known in the village as an educated man. His mother, the daughter of a freed slave from Africa, could neither read nor write.

When Sadat was young, his father and mother continued to live far away in neighboring Sudan. As a result, the children were raised by their grandmother in the village of Mit Abul-Kum. Sadat's grandmother, Sitt Om Muhammed, was well respected in the village, as she knew all the ancient Arab remedies to treat illness. She often told young Sadat stories of Arab heroes, who fought as best they could against the British, the rulers of Egypt at the time.

The British had occupied Egypt since 1882. They were cruel to the native people and treated them as inferiors and as slaves. If the Egyptians protested, they were whipped or even killed. The British made no effort to improve the lives of the Egyptians. There were very few schools and as a result the people were uneducated. Sadat grew up with a deep hatred for the British invaders.

One story, which was Sadat's favorite, stayed with him all his life. It was about Zahran, the hero from a village only three miles away from Mit Abul-Kum. British soldiers were shooting pigeons close to a tall silo of wheat. One of their bullets accidentally hit the silo and a fire started. The frightened soldiers ran from the scene. The farmers were enraged about their lost wheat and gathered together. One soldier shot a bullet at the farmers, and a bloody fight resulted in the soldier being killed.

The British could not have the commoners killing one of their soldiers, so they quickly arrested the offending farmers and put them on trial. They were found guilty, and some farmers were whipped and others were sentenced to be hung.

Because Zahran was the hero of the farmers, he was the first to walk up the platform to the gallows. He held his head high, proud and unafraid because he knew he had stood up to the enemy. Sadat often thought of Zahran and his heroism. Sadat wrote in his autobiography that as a young man he would say, "I wish I were Zahran."

Sadat inherited his mother's tight curly hair and dark skin, but his grandmother made sure that, unlike his mother, Sadat received an education at a very young age. She made him join the Koranic Teaching School, where he learned to read and write. He also had to be able to recite the entire Koran, the Holy Scripture of the Islamic religion.

The Koran is said to have been revealed to Muhammad, the founder of the Islamic religion, by Allah, or God. It is

The native Egyptians were often mistreated by British soldiers, and rioting became common in Egypt after the British took control of the country in 1882.

separated by *suras,* or chapters. The ability to recite the entire Koran is an important part of worship to the Islamic religion. The Koran teaches a person of Islamic faith who the true God is, and provides instructions about how to live, interact with others, and worship.

While learning, Sadat sat on the floor with his fellow students. He wore an *abayya,* an Arab garment, which had a deep pocket. Inside the pocket, he stored bread crusts and cheese to nibble on during his day at school.

After attending the Koranic Teaching School, his grand-mother sent him to Coptic Christian School. The Coptic Church is the native Christian church of Egypt and Ethiopia. Its churches are filled with colorful pictures of Bible stories painted on the walls. These paintings are used to teach illiterate people Bible stories. He did not stay there long, but in his auto-biography he remembered his teachers with fondness and fear.

When Sadat was not in school, he enjoyed the village life. He looked forward to sowing seeds, irrigation time, and harvest celebrations. He attended village wedding festivals and loved to eat *Kunafah*, a dessert pastry shaped like shoelaces and stuffed with sweet white cheese, nuts, and syrup. There were mango, orange, and berry orchards. He would pick cotton and then barter with the women who sold dates. Sadat recalled in his autobiography, "My life in the village was a succession of pleasant discoveries."

Throughout Sadat's life he referred back to the six years he spent in his beloved village. When he won the Nobel Peace Prize, he gave all the proceeds to Mit Abul-Kum. Later in life, Sadat made plans to retire to his little village. He began build-ing a house that overlooked the Nile Delta, but his dreams would never be fulfilled.

During the time Sadat lived in the village, the British ended their protection and control of Egypt. They recognized the Kingdom of Egypt and placed a "puppet" king, Fuad I, in power. King Fuad did not have the Egyptians' best interest in mind. Instead, he was willing to do whatever the British told him to do.

Sadat's village life ended abruptly when he was seven years old and his father moved the family to Cairo, the capital of Egypt. Sadat continued his studies in Cairo. His father paid for him to enroll in a private school called the Islamic Benevolent Society School. While walking to school every day, Sadat passed the Al-Qubbah Palace, one of the palaces of King Fuad. The first signs of Sadat's brazen personality were exhibited when he

The village of Mit Abul-Kum, where Sadat was raised by his grand-mother, is located in the Nile Delta. This area contains fertile land where farmers grow crops ranging from cotton to fruit trees.

and his friends stole apricots from the palace orchards. If they were caught, it could mean death.

Sadat did well in school and passed all his primary school exams. In 1930 he and his older brother, Tal'at, enrolled in the Fuad I Secondary School. Sadat's father gave him and his brother each £16 to pay for their schooling. This was difficult for his father as he made only £16 a month. Sadat used the money to go to school, but his brother took off and spent his. The brother then came home and announced he did not intend to go to school. Sadat reflected later in life that maybe this was destiny. If his brother had gone to school, his father could never have continued to pay for both of them.

Secondary school taught Sadat a lesson about social classes. His fellow classmates were the sons of government ministers and arrived at school by car. They wore fine suits and lived in beautiful homes. They could afford to buy chocolates and candies from the school store. Even so, Sadat was never envious. He was proud of the village where he had been born, and the lessons that he had learned there had made him feel confident.

Sadat was raised in poverty. His father had to support 13 children on his small income. Even though they lived in Cairo where bread could be bought in a store, Sadat only ate bread baked in the huge oven of their small home. He had a small allowance for lunch that was enough to buy a cup of milky tea.

Sadat got used to living in the big city of Cairo, but he often thought of and missed his village. Certain aspects of the city annoyed and disturbed him; for example, he hated the British police for driving through town like madmen on their motorcycles.

The first time Sadat saw a movie in a theater it was a terrible experience. A train on the screen seemed to be headed straight for him. He ran for his life. Before rushing out, he looked back at the screen—the train had disappeared. Instead a man and a woman were calmly sitting in a café. Sadat quietly went back to his seat.

When school let out, Sadat always traveled back to his village. During one summer vacation, Sadat heard that Hitler had marched from Munich to Berlin to regain land lost by the Germans during World War I. Inspired, Sadat gathered his friends and urged them to march from Mit Abul-Kum to Cairo to remove the British and regain Egypt as their own. His friends just laughed and walked away.

After Sadat completed secondary schooling, he decided to

join the Royal Military Academy. But before he could join, his father had to get a highly placed official's name as a reference for Sadat. His father remembered a friend from Sudan who could arrange a meeting with Major-General Ibrahim Khayri Pasha. The title "pasha" indicated that this man was a high official.

Sadat wrote about the day in his autobiography. His father had to stand in the hallway and wait for the pasha to pass by. After the pasha was informed as to who they were, he walked by them mumbling, "Oh yes. You're the senior clerk of the Health Department, and that's your son who . . . I see . . . all right, all right!" Sadat's father was a bit confused by the Pasha's words because he was merely a clerk in a military hospital, but they had gotten their reference. Sadat was enrolled in the prestigious Royal Military Academy. It was during Sadat's years at the academy that fate would bring him into contact with Gamal Abdel Nasser through the Free Officers' Organization. Many years later, Sadat, along with this group of men, would liberate Egypt from the British.

Sadat began his military career when he was granted admission to the prestigious Royal Military Academy in Cairo.

2

The Free Officers' Organization

Sadat graduated from the Royal Military Academy in 1938 and was stationed in Manqabad, a town in southern Egypt. He was commissioned as a second lieutenant in the Egyptian army. Just because Sadat had become a soldier, it did not mean that he agreed with the imposing British, quite the opposite. He wanted his fellow soldiers to understand the situation. Many of them were uneducated, so Sadat tirelessly taught them Egyptian history and showed them how the current government was not in Egypt's best interest. They drank tea and talked for hours. Sadat's room became known as the "National Assembly." During his time in Manqabad, the outpost was visited by Aziz al-Masri Pasha, the inspector general of the Egyptian army. Al-Masri took the group to a local monastery to show them a different culture. Sadat was deeply impressed by al-Masri because he had a long history of struggling for freedom and he also practiced cultural tolerance and understanding.

After al-Masri's visit, Sadat ordered books to learn about different cultures. While Sadat's friends went to movies in their free time, Sadat sat in a café and would read for hours while smoking a *hookah*, a vase like pipe where smoke is drawn through water.

The meetings in Sadat's room continued, and they eventually attracted the attention of Gamal Abdel Nasser. Sadat noticed that Nasser was extremely serious and distant. Most of the men stayed away from Nasser, but Sadat took an interest in him. However, at this point Sadat did not establish a close relationship with Nasser.

Sadat was then transferred to the Signal Corps in Maadi. Excited, he organized more meetings in the new location. This time many army officers joined. In 1939 the first secret army organization, the Free Officers' Organization, was established.

At this time, Sadat began planning the battle to overthrow the British government and give Egypt back to its people. Some of the soldiers also belonged to another organization called the Muslim Brotherhood. They also wanted to rid Egypt of the British, but their objectives were different from those of the Free Officers' Organization. The Muslim Brotherhood rejected all Western ideas and values. Its purposes were to consolidate all Islamic groups and enforce Islamic law. The Israelis were the prime enemy of the Muslim Brotherhood.

At first, Sadat was fascinated by the leader of the Muslim Brotherhood, Sheik al-Banna. But he found the reverence shown to him by his men despicable. Sadat finally confronted the sheik and bluntly told him that the Free Officers' Organization would not answer to any group except the people of Egypt.

On the personal side, Sadat wed at the age of 22 in

November 1940. His wife, Ekbal Madi, was also from his childhood village of Mit Abul-Kum. After the three-day wedding ceremony, the new couple moved to Cairo.

In the early 1940s, World War II was ravaging Europe. Italy had joined forces with Nazi Germany and started to advance on Egypt's neighboring country, Libya. The British forced the Egyptian army to defend Egypt's western desert from the advancing Nazis. The Egyptians did not see the Nazis as enemies, but rather as their deliverers from the British. German General Erwin Rommel seemed like a hero to them. The Egyptians shouted in the streets, "Advance Rommel!" The British, afraid the Egyptian army would turn on them instead of fighting the Nazis, ordered all Egyptians soldiers to put down their weapons and leave the western desert area.

In the summer of 1941, Sadat saw his opportunity to overthrow the British and started to plan the revolution. His idea was to get all the withdrawing soldiers to meet at the Mena House Hotel in Cairo. Once assembled, they would devise a scheme to overthrow the British in Cairo. Sadat arrived at the designated spot with his troops. He waited all night and the next day, but no other soldiers arrived. All of Sadat's plans and dreams had come to nothing.

Later that year, Sadat was contacted by his old friend, Aziz al-Masri. The British had dismissed al-Masri because of his anti-British sentiments. Al-Masri had been contacted by the Germans and asked to help with a battle in Iraq against the British. The Germans had arranged an airplane for al-Masri in an obscure location near Cairo. Sadat offered to drive him to the plane. Al-Masri agreed, so Sadat purchased a truck to transport his friend. Because of Sadat's relationship with al-Masri, he came under suspicion by the British. Sadat was transferred to another location, al-Garawlah, and was unable to help al-Masri. British intelligence discovered that al-Masri was headed to Iraq and had him arrested. Sadat was also arrested because of his connection to al-Masri.

Sadat was interrogated about his relationship with al-Masri. He told the prosecutor that his relationship with al-Masri was based on love and friendship. He was asked if he knew anything about al-Masri's connections to the Germans. Sadat told them that he had been in al-Garawlah, 340 miles away, so how could he possibly know of such a connection? The prosecutor ordered Sadat to be released, as there was not enough evidence to hold him. Sadat became deeply impressed by the British rules of law and their justice system. He realized that if his arrest had happened in any other country during a war, he could have simply been shot.

However, Sadat was determined to enlist Germany's help to overcome the British. He composed a message to General Rommel telling him that the Free Officers' Organization was on Germany's side. They would provide pictures of British troop positions to the Germans and help them win Egypt if after the war, Egypt was given complete independence. Sadat tried to contact Rommel via a colleague, but the colleague's plane was shot down.

Frantic to contact the general before Cairo was captured, Sadat became friends with two German spies. The spies gave Sadat a transmitter, which would allow him to transmit a message to General Rommel. The German spies did not seem serious about the war. They often visited the Kit Kat Nightclub, and money flowed freely as they partied the night away. Their wads of cash attracted attention. One of the dancers at the club reported the two men to the British authorities and they were soon arrested. During their interrogation, they mentioned Sadat's name, and in the middle of the night Sadat was taken into detention to await trial.

Using his earlier tactics, Sadat denied everything. He was confronted with the spies, and he told the jury that he thought they were British officers. The spies played along

German General Erwin Rommel is seen here talking to soldiers in Libya during Germany's North African campaign.

with Sadat. While Sadat was still in prison, Winston Churchill, the prime minister of England, visited Egypt and spoke to the spies. He told them that if they confessed everything, their lives would be spared. The spies confessed everything, including that Sadat had tried to contact General Rommel.

Sadat was then stripped of his officer status in the army. He was then arrested and transferred to the Alien's Jail. The Alien's Jail was only for prisoners connected with the war.

The cells were comfortable, with a bed, a blanket, and a small table. Smoking was allowed even though a warden had to light the cigarette, as prisoners were not allowed to have matches. Inmates were given two breaks a day and some used the time to walk inside the prison.

When Sadat was being taken to his cell, he later recalled in his autobiography, "I was overwhelmed by a strange joy—the joy of acknowledging a vast inner strength which I alone recognized. I had won, just as Zahran had won, although he was hanged and I was stripped of my rank and arrested."

During his time in jail, Sadat spent hours upon hours in self-reflection. He was confused and concerned about his future until he remembered the joy and happiness he felt in his childhood village. He realized that just having a small plot of land would satisfy him. Sadat also decided to improve his English, so he asked for newspapers and books. He devoured them and accumulated ideas on government management.

The cold winter months were beginning to wear on Sadat. One day, he received a package from home. Inside the package was a warm wool dressing gown. Sadat was ecstatic. He had been feeling isolated and homesick. The gown showed that someone still cared for him. Being deeply religious, he knelt on the ground and gave a thanksgiving prayer. As the years passed, Sadat's forehead grew a small bump from pressing his head on the ground to pray.

Over the next two years, Sadat was moved from one detention center to another. At one center, Sadat met a German prisoner who taught him how to read and speak German. Many years later, when Sadat was president, he would visit Austria and give a speech in German.

After the Allies won the war against Germany, Sadat became more restless. Something needed to be done about the British intrusion in Egypt. Sadat became frustrated, being locked up behind the prison walls, powerless and unable to help his country. He needed to escape. Finally,

Sadat was moved to a detention center in Cairo where he formed a plan.

Along with five other prisoners, Sadat planned to leave the prison through a hole in the ceiling. They successfully escaped but were caught shortly after. During their trial, they complained of ill-treatment. Their treatment improved, but Sadat did not want to be in prison any longer. He staged a hunger strike and was transferred to a hospital. Sadat and another prisoner escaped during the busy lunch hour. They walked quickly through the crowd before the guards could notice them and jumped into a waiting car. Sadat was free, but now he would have to hide from the authorities. He grew a beard and used the name of Hadji Muhammad. He took any job he could get, such as loading trucks or hauling rocks from docked ships to construction sites.

World War II ended on May 7, 1945. The Germans surrendered, and the British lifted martial laws, the temporary laws during wartime. These laws were the reason Sadat had been arrested in the first place. Now that they were lifted, Sadat was a free man.

Still as determined as ever to overthrow the British, Sadat quickly got back to forming a secret organization. He felt the only way to get the British to leave was through violence. Sadat approached Gamal Nasser with his ideas, but Nasser refused to get involved. However, there were others who felt the same way as Sadat, and they planned to assassinate Mustafa el-Nahas, Egypt's wartime prime minister. El-Nahas agreed with British policies and therefore was considered a traitor.

The plan was to throw a grenade at el-Nahas's car as he drove to make a scheduled speech. One of the members of the secret organization, Hussein Tewfik, was appointed to throw the grenade. He threw the grenade too early, and it missed el-Nahas's car by seconds. The plan had failed. They regrouped and decided to assassinate Amin Osman Pasha,

On May 7, 1945, German Field Marshal Wilhelm Keitel signed the terms of surrender in Berlin. At the end of World War II, Britain lifted martial law in Egypt.

the leader of the Revival League. This league asserted that there was a marriage of sorts between the British government and Egypt and that the union could never be dissolved. Sadat was horrified by these principles and felt it was his duty to eradicate the organization.

Again Hussein Tewfik was appointed to carry out the assassination. Tewfik executed the plan with accuracy and Amin Osman's dead body lay on the sidewalk. Tewfik was later identified by an Egyptian air force officer who saw him pull the trigger.

Tewfik gave a full confession, including Sadat's part in the assassination. On a January night in 1946, Sadat was arrested and taken to Alien's Jail. He stayed there briefly until he was transferred to Cell 54. The conditions were harsh and inhumane, but it was within the walls of Cell 54 that Sadat would draw on his inner strength.

Sadat was released from Cairo Central Prison and moved to Suez to start a new life.

3

The Revolution

Sadat arrived at Cairo Central Prison in January 1946 and was led to Cell 54. The luxuries he experienced in Alien's Jail were nonexistent in his new cell. There was no bed or table, only a small stony concrete floor with a palm mat on the ground. Crumbled in the corner was a dirty blanket that looked as though it had never been washed. There were no books to read or paper to write on. There was no radio to listen to and no companionship for the 18 months Sadat lived in the cell.

During the winter months, water seeped through the cell walls, and a freezing wind chilled Sadat. In the summer, Sadat had to share his cell with throngs of bugs that walked along the wet floor. There was a hole, which served as a window.

His case was still under review, and he had not yet been convicted. Therefore, Sadat was put in solitary confinement so he would not have to mix with the other hardened criminals. In his autobiography, Sadat wrote about solitary confinement, "In Cell 54 I could only be my own companion . . . it was only natural that I should come to know that "self" of mine. . . . A barrier seemed to stand between us. There were areas of suffering which kept that "self" in the dark. . . . One of these was my marriage."

He realized that he had grown apart from his wife. The marriage had been arranged, and he had nothing in common with her. Sadat had put off his feelings of doubt for years because of the values he had been taught while growing up. But now with so much time on his hands, the thoughts were nagging and persistent. He knew that his destiny was going to lead him to public life, and his wife would not be able to cope with it. He told his wife to stop visiting him and decided once he was released he was going to ask for a divorce.

This decision gave Sadat a feeling of peace. He wrote, "Nothing is more important than self-knowledge. Once I had come to know what I wanted, and got rid of what I didn't, I was reconciled to my 'self' and learned to live at peace with it."

Trouble in Palestine started while Sadat was behind prison walls. As a result of World War II, large groups of German Jews fled Europe and found safety in Palestine. The residing Arabs were furious about the influx of immigrants and began attacking the arriving Jews. The United Nations was called in to stop the attacks. It dissolved the country of Palestine and decided to split it into two states, an Arab state and a Jewish state. The Arab state was the West Bank of the Jordan River, now called Jordan, and the Egyptian controlled Gaza Strip, a small piece of land on the Mediterranean Sea. The rest of Palestine was a Jewish state called Israel. Jerusalem was the only city to be considered neutral because of the many holy places for Muslims, Jews, and Christians within its boundaries. These places would be available for all to visit.

Israeli Prime Minister David Ben Gurion (left) signed the United Nations document that dissolved Palestine and split it into an Arab state and the Jewish state of Israel.

The Jewish population was in favor of the United Nations decree, as they now had their own country. But the Arabs ignored it and asserted the United Nations had no right to split up their land. The first Arab-Israeli war broke out in May 1948.

In 1964 a group called the Palestine Liberation Organization (PLO) was formed. The sole purpose of this group was to completely dissolve Israel. Prior to the formation of this group, there was no such thing as a Palestinian. There were only Palestinian Arabs and Palestinian Jews. Arabs and Jews worked side by side and were even friends. All this stopped when members of the PLO started harassing and even killing Arabs who were sympathetic toward their Jewish neighbors.

Meanwhile, Sadat's case was finally taken to trial. It dragged on for many days. Sadat had the best lawyers in Egypt defending him, and in early July 1948 he was found not guilty. After his release, Sadat was uncertain about his future. He moved to Hilwan and drank the local mineral water to soothe his damaged digestive system. Sadat quickly ran out of money and luckily received an unexpected visitor while he was performing his morning prayers. An old friend, Hassan Issat, asked Sadat to live with him in the city of Suez. Sadat quickly gathered his belongings. His clothes were so threadbare that Hassan suggested they stop and buy some new clothes for Sadat.

In Hassan's home, Sadat met Jehan. She was Hassan's wife's cousin and visited often. Sadat and Jehan spent a lot of time together.

Sadat soon realized that Hassan had not asked Sadat to come to Suez out of friendship. Hassan needed help with a trading business that involved the Saudis. Hassan promised Sadat a certain percentage of the deal. Sadat quickly got to work and struck a profitable deal with the Saudis. Once the business transaction was finalized, Sadat calculated his percentage to be 180 sovereigns. But Hassan only gave Sadat 60 and pocketed the rest.

After being deceived by Hassan in this business deal, Sadat found a job in publishing. During that time he proposed to Jehan. On September 29, 1948, Jehan's father accepted the proposal, and Jehan and Sadat were married eight months later.

The couple moved to Zaqaziq, and Sadat set up another business with Hassan, this time providing drinking water to villages. He worked long hard hours and the company cleared about $45,000. Sadat asked Hassan for an apartment and stability for his new family. Hassan replied that Sadat had already taken his share out of the company, which was a lie. Sadat was completely sickened by Hassan's behavior and later recalled in *In Search of Identity*, "All I wanted was to get away—to save myself. Indeed, money would be worthless if it posed a threat to man's real entity, his inner peace and mental life."

Sadat realized that his dream was not to be a businessman. He felt the only way to accomplish his mission in life was to go back to the army. He had been absolved of all blame for his crime, so he was allowed to rejoin. Sadat became an army captain on January 15, 1950. Soon Gamal Abdel Nasser called Sadat to congratulate him. Nasser had taken command of the Free Officers' Organization while Sadat was in prison and quickly updated Sadat on the organization's growth. It had become quite powerful in Egypt. Nasser had divided the organization into groups of cells. Each cell was unaware of the other cell. That way if one cell was discovered, they could not be forced to confess the plans of the other cells. Nasser set up a governing council for the Free Officers' Organization and Sadat was chosen to be on it. The council's main objectives were to overthrow King Farouk, rid Egypt of the British, and establish a true Egyptian government.

During this time, Sadat met Yasir Arafat, who eventually became the leader of the PLO. In Janet and John Wallach's *Arafat, In the Eyes of the Beholder,* Arafat remembered his earlier association with the Free Officers' Organization. He said, "We began to make contacts with the Egyptian officers and they used to give us weapons and ammunition."

The council for the Free Officers' Organization met in January 1952 and set a date for the revolution, November 1955. Just days after the Free Officers' Organization meeting, a huge riot, called the "Cairo fire," took place in Cairo on January 26. A violent expression of frustration broke out among Egyptians. Years of subjugation and suffering were brought to the

Egyptians demanded that the British leave their military posts at the Suez Canal. This protest in 1951 came after Egyptian soldiers were killed in a conflict with the British at the Suez Canal.

forefront. No one knew who started the riot, but the council decided to rethink the date of their revolution.

They needed more information regarding the king. So, Sadat contacted a good friend of his, the king's private physician. Sadat learned that the king was very disturbed by the recent rioting. The king felt uncertain as to his future in Egypt and even started to smuggle gold out of the country.

The Free Officers' Organization council convened again in February 1952. Sadat relayed what was told to him by the physician. The council decided to execute the revolution plans in November 1952.

A few months after the February meeting, Nasser discovered through a journalist friend that the king was planning to appoint a tough new war minister who knew all about the Free Officers' Organization. The minister's first objective was to disband the group. Nasser changed the date of the revolution again—this time he planned it for July 1952, which was before the new war minister could take office.

On July 21, 1952, Sadat was stationed at Al-Arish. He received an urgent message from Nasser to go to Cairo immediately. The revolution was to take place between July 22 and August 5. Sadat arrived by train in Cairo on July 22. Nasser was not there to meet him. Sadat thought he had arrived in Cairo too early. He then went to his house and took his wife out to the movies. When Sadat and his wife returned after 10:00 P.M., there were two urgent messages from Nasser for Sadat. The revolution was to take place that night. Was he going to miss the revolution? Would he be known as just a bystander and not a soldier of the revolution he had dreamed of since he was a child?

Quickly Sadat changed into his army clothes and headed to the Al-Abbasiah army barracks. As shots whizzed through the air, Sadat tried to tell a soldier to let him in. The soldier did not believe that Sadat was part of the revolution, so he refused. A friend heard Sadat's voice and was able to come to his rescue. Inside Sadat found Nasser and was told that the army barracks had already been secured and top military officers had been arrested.

Nasser informed Sadat that the revolution had to be started immediately, as King Farouk's guards had learned of Nasser's plans. Guards were being posted throughout the army barracks to protect them from the Free Officers'

Organization. They had to act immediately. He then asked Sadat to call each of the unit commanders throughout Egypt—Sinai, the Western Desert, Alexandria, and Rafa. Sadat's calming voice reassured the commanders on the other end of the phone, thereby helping the revolution proceed smoothly. Sadat informed Nasser and the other members of the council that all had gone as planned.

Sadat stood on the balcony at the army barracks and admired the sunrise. Off in the distance, he watched as the men of the Free Officers' Organization boarded tanks and army trucks and headed into Cairo. The revolution had begun.

Sadat later recalled in his autobiography, "The dream on which I had lived for years—a dream to which I devoted my entire life—had finally materialized." He was filled with such joy and happiness that he wanted to share this with other people. He drove to the Broadcasting House to announce the revolution to the people of Egypt. Once he left the building, he saw people gathering in the streets. Men, women, and children were hugging, shaking hands, and kissing each other.

Meanwhile, King Farouk was in his summer house, Ras al-Tin Palace, in Alexandria, so the Free Officers' Organization marched toward the city. After two days, the Free Officers' took over the palace on July 26. The next step was to get rid of the king. Sadat was appointed to make it happen. He wrote an ultimatum and set up a meeting with the king. Sadat pulled out the ultimatum from his briefcase and read it out loud. The demands were, "The king should leave Egypt by six o'clock in the evening on July 26, 1952. If he failed to do so, he would have to bear all the consequences."

The king accepted the ultimatum. Sadat immediately contacted the royal yacht to tell them to prepare to sail the king and his family out of Egypt that evening. Sadat told the captain that the royal yacht was to be returned to Egypt once the king had been removed. Sadat also arranged for a few aircraft to give the yacht a flyover salute as it left Egyptian waters.

That evening at 6:00 P.M., Sadat stood on board Egypt's largest warship and watched the royal yacht pull away. The flyover salute warned the king and showed the world that the new government was self-confident, and filled with pride and determination. This was to be the new Egyptian government with Gamal Abdel Nasser at its helm.

Gamal Abdel Nasser led a movement to end the monarchy in Egypt. While Nasser was president, Egypt fought with the combined forces of Britain, France, and Israel for control of the Suez Canal.

4

President Gamal Abdel Nasser

G amal Nasser had a similar background to Sadat in that he was born in a small village, Beni Morr, in Upper Egypt. When he was young, he developed a deep hatred for the British. He took part in student demonstrations where he was hit by police batons. In one demonstration he was shot in the forehead, and the scar stayed with him for life.

Nasser admired men of leadership including Adolf Hitler because Hitler had stood up to the British. According to David Hirst and Irene Beeson's *Sadat,* Nasser asked in a letter to a friend, "Where is the man who can rebuild the country so that the weak and humiliated Egyptian can stand up again and live free and independent?"

After the revolution, Nasser gave the Free Officers' Organization council a new name, the Revolutionary Command Council. Nasser was unanimously elected as the chairman of the new council.

recalled in his autobiography, "We also reject the Mutual Security Pact because it affects our independence, which we value as highly as life itself."

Shots were being fired between Israel and Egypt along the Gaza Strip. Outpost soldiers were being killed. Egyptian soldiers made demands for better weapons. Nasser and the council decided to approach the Soviet Union in 1953. Joseph Stalin, the premier of the U.S.S.R., refused to sell weapons to a non-Communistic country. Stalin died in 1953, and two years later the first arms deal was struck with the Soviet Union and Czechoslovakia.

In 1954 the council got the British government to sign the Evacuation Agreement. After 75 years, the British flag was removed and the new Egyptian flag waved proudly in the air as the last British soldier left Egypt on June 19, 1956. However, one problem remained—a British and French company still controlled the Suez Canal.

On July 26, 1956, Nasser surprised the world by announcing that the Suez Canal now belonged to the Egyptian people. During his speech, Egyptian soldiers were executing Nasser's plan to take over the canal company offices. Soldiers with guns drawn ousted the current occupants. Sadat was appalled at this brash move, as the arms had not even been delivered from the Soviet Union. Sadat said in *In Search of Identity* that he told Nasser, "If you had consulted me, I would have told you to be more careful. This step means war, and we are not ready for it."

Was Nasser going to lose everything gained this far? The French and British governments set meetings to negotiate with Egypt that went on for several months. But in the background, they had representatives meeting with Israel, and on October 29, 1956, the combined forces struck. Air-raid sirens screamed through the streets of Cairo. Nasser scrambled to the roof of his home and saw airplanes with British and French markings flying overhead. They bombed all the aircraft recently purchased from the Soviet Union. Egypt approached the Soviet Union to help

British diplomat Anthony Nutting (left) and Nasser signed the agreement that ended Britain's occupation of the Suez Canal area.

them fight the French, British, and Israeli invaders. Soviet officials absolutely refused.

On November 5, President Dwight D. Eisenhower made a speech in the United States regarding the Middle East situation. He said that the United States could not impose one law for the weak and another for the strong; one law for those allied with the United States and another for those opposed. There was only one law and that was peace. Eisenhower presented a cease-fire resolution to the United Nations and won majority support. France and Britain were ordered to withdraw. Israel also withdrew, as the United States was their strongest ally.

Egypt was now in control of the Suez Canal, the 100-mile stretch of water from the Mediterranean Sea to the Red Sea, which eventually met the Indian Ocean. Israel was no longer allowed to sail ships through it, thereby making Israel's only route to the Indian Ocean through the Strait of Tiran just outside the Gulf of Aqaba.

Sadat felt that this was now the time for Egypt to establish a relationship with the United States. Nasser, however, completely disregarded the help of the United States and continued to praise the Soviet Union. Sadat felt that Nasser's view was becoming influenced by the men under him. Their only purpose was to flatter Nasser and make themselves look good to get a promotion.

As time went by, Sadat filled more and more roles in the government. From 1954 to 1956, Sadat served as the minister of state. Then in 1957, he was appointed secretary general of the National Union. But Nasser and Sadat's relationship started to cool. Sadat assumed that Nasser had heard slanderous remarks about him and believed what Sadat's enemies were saying.

Suddenly on May 15, 1960, Sadat suffered a heart attack. Nasser quickly came to his friend's side, and they discussed their differences and became trusted friends once again.

In the early 1960s, Egypt's financial situation started to deteriorate. Public utilities had been ignored by the government. Egypt's telephone system, public transportation, and housing were in a state of disrepair. Uprisings became common among the students, and the Muslim fundamentalists formed another plot to assassinate Nasser. A huge crackdown was executed by the government to quell the dissatisfaction.

At this time, the Arab world looked to Egypt to handle the problems in Palestine. Arafat remembers in *Arafat, In the Eyes of the Beholder,* "Nasser invited thirteen Arab leaders to the First Arab Summit [1964] in Cairo . . . he declared that there should be an official Palestinian group to fight the Israelis. Its political arm was to be called the Palestine Liberation Organization. . . . Its military side would be named the Palestine Liberation Army."

Nasser was heavily criticized by the Arab world for allowing Israeli ships to pass through the Strait of Tiran. He called Egypt's council together to discuss the possibility of closing the strait. Sadat recalled the council meeting in his autobiography: Nasser informed the council, "If we close the Strait, war will be a one hundred percent certainty." He then turned and asked the commander-in-chief of the armed forces, Abdel Hakim Amer, if the Egyptian army was ready for a war. "Amer pointed to his neck and said: 'On my own head be it, boss! Everything's in tiptop shape.'"

Everyone, including Sadat, voted to close the strait. On June 2, 1967, Nasser signed the Defensive War Plan. On Monday, June 5, Amer decided to make an aerial inspection of the Egyptian Sinai troops and positions. He ordered Egyptian antiaircraft guns to hold fire while he was in the air. While Amer was in his aircraft, the Israelis suddenly attacked all the Egyptian airfields and demolished all the aircraft on the ground.

Sadat, unaware that there was any problem, was at home when he heard the news that Israel had started an attack. In his autobiography, he remembers thinking at the time, "Well, they'll be taught a lesson they won't forget." He took his time changing his clothes and calmly drove to command headquarters. When he arrived at 11:00 A.M., Amer was there. Sadat greeted Amer cheerfully, confident of Egypt's success in the battle. Amer seemed confused and did not reply. That's when Sadat realized that the attack had been more significant than he had initially thought.

Once Sadat learned of Egypt's losses, he was devastated. Not only had Israel destroyed Egypt's air force, but they had also captured part of its territory. Israel gained control of the Gaza Strip, the Sinai Peninsula, East Jerusalem, the Golan Heights in Syria, and the West Bank of the Jordan River. What would become known as the Six-Day War had begun.

Sadat slowly drove home and stayed inside for days. His sense of loss was further aggravated by false media reports. The radio blared lies of Egypt's successes in the Six-Day War. People shouted for joy and danced in the streets celebrating an imagined victory. Sadat resented that Nasser had not done anything about the poor military tactics issued by Amer.

Tension in the Middle East was escalating in 1967, and would eventually erupt in the Six-Day War. These Israeli tank crews underwent many training exercises during this time to ensure that they were ready for battle.

Nasser prepared a speech, and on June 9, 1967, he stood before the people of Egypt. He told them that the United States had issued the attack and wanted to control the world and rule Egypt just like the British. He could not grant such a wish, therefore he was stepping down as president. The streets were crammed with people listening to him. Almost in unison they cried out and pleaded with Nasser to stay. He decided to bow to their wishes and remained as president.

As a result of the Six-Day War, Egyptians had lost their hope, pride, and honor. Nasser burned with revenge after the sore defeat to Israel, so in 1968 he began a War of Attrition with the intent to wear down the enemy. Instead, when the Egyptians launched a bomb to the Israeli side, the Israeli's launched one back. If the Egyptians built their barricade high, the Israelis would build theirs higher.

After the Six-Day War, Nasser's health started to deteriorate. His diabetes was out of control for five months. Then he developed sores all over his body. They were so tender he could not even put on his clothes. He was given a medication for nervous tension to get rid of the sores, but then pain developed in his legs.

In September 1969, Nasser suffered a heart attack. Nasser became concerned about his country's future, as he thought it was likely he would die. Nasser spoke to Sadat on December 16, 1969, before Nasser was to leave on a trip to Morocco. Nasser appointed Sadat vice president, and he was sworn in before Nasser's trip.

On September 28, 1970, Nasser was at home resting. He was scheduled to meet Sadat later that evening. Sadat received a phone call to come to Nasser's house immediately. When he arrived, he was shown to Nasser room. He was then informed by the attending physicians that Nasser had died. Sadat could not believe it. According to *In Search of Identity*, Sadat turned to the doctors and said: "'It's not true. . . . What you're saying is wrong. . . . It can't be right!' They said they had done everything possible . . . but the will of God could not be reversed."

Sadat addressed the National Assembly after Nasser's funeral. Less than a month after Nasser died, Sadat was elected president.

5

Sadat Takes Charge

E gypt was shaken to the core by the death of their beloved leader. Throughout the Arab world, people poured into the streets weeping and wailing.

Sadat was reluctant to become the next Egyptian president and announced that he would carry on as the vice president. He soon regretted this decision, as there were many rivalries to the presidential position. He received letters from neighboring countries stating that Egypt needed a valid president. Also, the Egyptian armed forces demanded a supreme commander to lead them. So immediately after Nasser's funeral, Sadat summoned the top officials in the government and told them he had changed his decision. He wanted a presidential election right away and on October 15, 1970, Anwar Sadat was elected president.

After attending Nasser's funeral, U.S. diplomats reported to

President Richard Nixon that Sadat would not last for more than four to six weeks as Egypt's president. Earlier in Sadat's career, he always appeared in Nasser's shadow. His way of handling Nasser had given Sadat the image of a pushover.

Immediately after taking office, Sadat informed the Egyptian people that 1971 would be the "Year of Decision." He immediately went about changing Nasser's old domestic policies. On his first day as president, Nasser's minister for presidential affairs handed Sadat a stack of papers. "What is this?" he asked.

"The text of tapped telephone conversations between certain people being watched."

Sadat wrote in his autobiography that after this conversation he ordered the minister to stop tapping citizen's phone conversations. He then swept the papers off his desk.

During Nasser's reign, a cultivation of fear arose among the common people. Sadat became acutely aware of this and immediately set about to change this idea. According to author Raphael Israeli, "Sadat had said once that to be gripped by fear was the most degrading of all emotions for a human being. In fear, personality disintegrates, the human will is paralyzed and man acts as an automaton." Sadat became known as the ruler that was sensible and good-humored, like an easygoing father figure.

He also found that Egypt's international relations were at an all-time low. The only country that Egypt had any relations with at all was the Soviet Union. Nasser's emotions alienated Egypt to the rest of the world. If he was given any negative report, true or false, from one of his men, Nasser would immediately think it was true. He would attack the country involved in the alleged incident. These actions further isolated Egypt.

Sadat called the minister of finance and economy into his office and asked him about Egypt's economic situation. Sadat recalled in his autobiography, "He said simply that the treasury was empty and we were almost bankrupt." It was so bad that soldiers on the front lines and civil servants were not receiving pay.

Nasser had integrated a socialist budget, which stifled free enterprise. Thus the government was responsible for providing everything to citizens—food, work, housing, and education. There were no incentives to work or be productive. All private property belonged to the state under Nasser's direction. Sadat immediately placed the property back in the hands of the original owners. Soviet agents in Egyptian political circles strongly disagreed.

Sadat had to overcome horrendous obstacles to put Egypt back on the path of prosperity and pride. He often fell back on his deep faith in Allah and his childhood memories from his village, Mit Abul-Kum. One of his daughters, Rawiya, observed in *Man of Defiance*, "The most inspiring sight of my father was that of him at prayer: he seemed to be in direct communication with Allah."

Sadat's wife, Jehan, recalled that her husband was a very simple man. He did not like jewelry or anything adorning his body. He often fasted and only ate basic foods such as vegetables, fruit, and lean meat. He loved to go on long walks and would often gaze up into the sky in meditation. He insisted that the furnishings in his bedroom be very simple and when others were not at the house, he would sit on the floor. He viewed the peasant, the people of the land, as being closest to God.

On May 11, 1971, there was talk of drafting a new Egyptian constitution. According to *Man of Defiance*, Sadat told the Parliament, "When we draft the constitution, we ought to return to the village, where lie our roots. . . . Certainly the constitution is not just for the village, but I want it worded in such as way as to turn the whole of Egypt into one big village."

After finding out the status of Egypt, internationally and domestically, Sadat immediately got to work. His first order of business was to regain the land lost in the Six-Day War. Egypt's pride needed to be restored. He visited Moscow and insisted that the Soviets supply the missiles they had promised Nasser. The Soviet leadership approved the plan as long as Egyptians did not use the missiles unless they had Moscow's approval. Sadat flatly refused and left.

After Sadat became president, he returned to his childhood village of Mit Abul-Kum to pray in a mosque there.

Once he arrived in Cairo, he informed the Supreme Executive Council, which included a few Soviet agents, of the outcome of his talks with Moscow. The Soviet agents walked out of the room.

On May 20, 1971, Sadat was warned that there was going to be an attempt on his life. Sadat already knew that Soviet agents had been in disagreement with him from the start. Sadat immediately had all Soviet agents and sympathizers arrested or dismissed from service. He quickly replaced them with trusted men.

The Russian government was shocked by Sadat's move. Nikolai Podgorny, the president of the Soviet Union, immediately visited Egypt. A political cartoon was being circulated at the time that pictured Podgorny visiting his friends in Egypt, and they were all wearing prison uniforms.

Podgorny insisted Sadat sign a 15-year Treaty of Friendship and Cooperation. Sadat agreed, but first had some complaints to voice. He told Podgorny that he did not like the way Egypt was being treated by the Soviets. He would sign the treaty to prove his good intentions—but would Russia make good on their previous promises regarding the delivery of arms? Sadat wrote in his autobiography that Podgorny said, "Give me four days and all weapons you have asked for will be shipped to you." Sadat signed the treaty in good faith.

After Podgorny left, Sadat waited from June through September for the promised arms. He wrote letters and got no answers. Podgorny's promise had turned out to be empty words. Sadat visited Russia many times throughout 1971. According to *Man of Defiance*, finally in 1972, Sadat informed the Russian leader, Leonid Brezhnev, "I cannot accept this kind of treatment; if it continues, it will cause a very serious rift in our relationship." Still no arms arrived.

Eager to fight Israel over Egypt's lost land, Sadat persistently contacted Moscow for the promised arms. He knew that U.S. President Nixon would be visiting Moscow to discuss the Middle East. The Soviets promised Sadat a detailed report of the meeting. After the Nixon-Moscow meeting, Sadat was informed by Russia that both superpowers decided to have a relaxed attitude toward the Middle East. Sadat was furious.

He then received a letter from Soviet leaders on July 8th. Raphael Israeli included a portion of the letter in his book, "As to war, we are concerned about it. Waging wars, preparing for them and training for them is a very dangerous proposition. But it is useful to mention that you are unable at this point to launch a war."

Sadat's was further inflamed by Russia's attitude toward Egypt. He quickly wrote a response, which told the Soviets that he rejected their ideas and their way of doing things. From that point forward, he wanted all Soviet experts and installations removed from Egypt. Within one week, all Soviets in Egypt had left the country. Even so, Russia did not want to let go of Egypt that easily. Egypt had a strong Russian presence in the Arab world and therefore was useful to Russia in international relations. Finally in 1973, Sadat signed a new agreement with Moscow for military supplies. Some of the arms arrived in Egypt. Sadat could now proceed with his plans to regain the land lost in the Six-Day War.

He secretly met with Syrian President Hafez al-Assad to plan a combined attack on Israel. Syria had also lost territory in the Six-Day War and al-Assad was eager to get it back. The date was set for October 6, 1973, Yom Kippur, the holiest Jewish holiday. It was a Jewish day of fasting and making amends for past wrongs.

Like a game of crying wolf, Sadat spread misinformation to confuse Israel. In May, he released information that Egypt was planning to attack Israel. He ordered the military to set up as though going to war. Israel moved troops to prepare for a possible attack. None came. Sadat did the same thing in August. Each time Israel maneuvered troops for war, it cost them $10 million. By the time Israel got a report about an October attack, it was almost ignored.

In *Man of Defiance*, Raphael Israeli wrote about a visit that Sadat had with his daughter, Camellia, a few days before October 6. "Just before she departed, he asked her whether she had enough money; when she answered yes, he murmured, 'Be sure to stock up with sugar and oil.'" Camellia followed her father's advice certain that an emergency was going to happen.

At exactly 2:00 P.M. on October 6, 1973, 222 Egyptian supersonic jets took off and within 20 minutes they demolished the

Israeli command post, aerial combat headquarters, air defense, missiles and guns in the Sinai, and electronic-warfare equipment. They had hit 90 percent of their scheduled targets and lost only a few airplanes. Israel was in a state of shock and was taken completely by surprise. Sadat personally congratulated the Egyptian air force commander, General Hosni Mubarak. (At a later date, Sadat would ask Mubarak to leave the army and serve the country as vice president.)

After the surprise air strike, 3,000 field guns or cannons began to fire at the Israeli post on the east side of the Suez Canal. The blasts were the heaviest concentration of fire the world had ever experienced since World War II.

When the attack ended, the Egyptian soldiers enthusiastically pushed boats into the canal and crossed to the other side, shouting, "Allah is greater!" Once the soldiers arrived, they quickly scaled the 47-foot wall of sand erected by the Israelis and took over their command posts. A makeshift bridge was built and Egyptian troops poured across. Within six hours, Egypt's flag waved proudly in the air. Now the painful memories of the Six-Day War could be erased by the victory of the "Six-Hour War" in October 1973.

Army engineers were sent to the sand wall by the Suez Canal and started carving an opening into the wall. They used high-powered water pumps to cut through the sand like a knife. Tanks easily rolled over to the east bank of the Suez Canal further securing Egypt's position.

As Israeli reported in his book, Sadat informed the people of Egypt, "This is a war for our honor and self-respect. No one will defend my dignity and self-respect for me, for I am the ruler of the land and the bearer of its self-respect."

Sadat recalled in his autobiography, "I used to tell Nasser that if we could recapture even 4 inches of Sinai territory. . . . First to go would be the humiliation we had endured since the 1967 defeat; for, to cross into Sinai and hold on to any territory captured would restore our self-confidence."

The Egyptian army captured these Israeli soldiers during the
October 1973 war.

On the northern side of Israel, Syria heavily attacked
Israel's borders. Within three days, Israel had lost one-third of
its air force as well as many of its seasoned pilots. By the fourth
day, the highly respected and well-known Israeli commander,
General Abraham Mindler, was killed on the battlefield. Henry
Kissinger, the U.S. secretary of state, informed Israel's prime
minister, Golda Meir, that Egypt had won the war and to
prepare her country for defeat.

On that same day, Egypt completely demolished Israel's most
important unit, the Armored Brigade 190. The brigade was trying
to penetrate Egypt's forces and after only 20 minutes of battle all
120 Israeli tanks had been destroyed except for Commander Assaf
Yagouri's tank. Once the commander realized this, he had a
nervous breakdown and then surrendered to the Egyptian forces.

On October 13, seven days after the war, Sadat was given a

message from Kissinger to negotiate a cease-fire. Sadat recalled in *In Search of Identity* that his reply was, "I am willing to have a cease-fire if Israel agrees to withdraw from the occupied Arab territories." These terms were not acceptable to Israel, so instead the United States started supplying Israel with much needed tanks after their great losses. The United States was also providing Israel with hourly transmitted information via satellite regarding Egypt's army movements.

Sadat grew concerned with U.S. involvement and thought that the newly supplied Israel would be able to wipe out any gain Egypt had made. He knew they needed more weapons and supplies. He turned to the Russians for help and they refused. In desperation, he turned to other Arab nations and Yugoslavia to come to his rescue. That's when he found out who his true friends were. Yugoslavian President Tito shipped over 140 army tanks, fueled and ready to go. Sadat turned to the Shah of Iran and received a message that 600 tons of oil was on the way. Jordan, Saudi Arabia, and Iraq sent men and other war material. North Vietnam and North Korea sent pilots. However, when he asked the leader of Libya, Muammar Qaddafi, for oil. Several tankers left Egypt for Libya to be filled with oil; but they returned empty.

Meanwhile, Arab countries cut their oil supply to pro-Israel countries. "No Gas" signs popped up throughout the United States, Japan, and Europe. The Arab countries threatened to stop all shipments of oil to those countries if they did not change their policies toward Israel.

Sadat's popularity soared at home. On the 11th day of the war, Sadat drove to the Parliament building to address Egypt's National Assembly. Tens of thousands of people lined the streets of Cairo and cheered for their great leader. Radios and televisions all over Egypt were tuned in to hear Sadat speak. He told the Egyptian people that he fought for peace. All he wanted was for Israel to withdraw from all occupied territories. He then announced that he would like to clear and reopen the Suez Canal.

Egyptian soldiers show their support for Sadat before the October 22, 1973, cease-fire agreement.

6

The Hero of October

The war raged on, and Israel started to gain more ground. As a result, Sadat contacted Kissinger and ordered a cease-fire. Because Egypt received arms and support from Russia, it was considered to be under the Russian superpower's umbrella. Therefore, Kissinger contacted Moscow to hammer out the terms of the cease-fire.

On October 22, 1973, the cease-fire came into effect. It was presented to Egypt and Israel and was quickly signed, but within two hours after the signing, fighting resumed. Israel and Egypt each blamed the other for the violation. Israel attempted to enter the Suez Canal on its west bank. The soldiers were unsuccessful, but they managed to establish a four-mile gap along the east bank of the canal. Israel also surrounded the Egyptian Third Army, which consisted of 10,000 soldiers. Sadat ordered the army to heavily enforce the cities on the west bank. Frustrated, he got in touch with Russia and the United States. According to his autobiography, he said, "Please come in. I am willing to have your forces land on Egyptian territory to ensure that the Israelis pull back to the October 22 lines."

The Russians landed forces on the Mediterranean, while the United States announced the possibilities of nuclear war. That's when Sadat received a personal letter from President Nixon. In *Memoirs*, Nixon remembered his reply to Sadat's request, "Should the two great nuclear powers be called upon to provide forces, it would introduce an extremely dangerous potential for direct great-power rivalry in the area."

In November 1973, Kissinger arrived in Egypt to meet with Sadat to negotiate a disengagement agreement. Sadat recalled the conversation in his autobiography. Kissinger said, "You've created an international crisis, and that's why I've come to see you. What are your requests?"

"I want a return," Sadat replied, "to the cease-fire lines of October 22."

They talked for three hours. They finally agreed that Egyptian-Israeli talks for disengagement of forces would be held under United Nations supervision. The talks were to take place at Kilometer 101 on the Cairo-Suez road.

Moscow began to feel snubbed, as Sadat no longer contacted Soviet leaders to assist with the negotiations. He was working directly with the United States. Sadat viewed Egypt's relationship to Russia as though working with moving sand. He felt that the United States and its representatives were more solid and trustworthy.

On Tuesday, October 30, 1973, the talks began between Egypt and Israel. In the past, talks between Israel and an Arab nation had to have a go-between appointed. Anwar Sadat threw this tradition aside and allowed his representative to speak directly to Israel's spokesperson. Egypt demanded that Israel withdraw to the cease-fire lines. Israel insisted on the

U.S. Secretary of State Henry Kissinger played a key role in negotiations to stop Arab-Israeli fighting. He also helped end the Arab oil embargo against the United States.

return of their prisoners before any withdrawal took place. Arguments broke out between Egypt and Israel, and Sadat asked for the talks to be suspended.

As Kissinger recalled in his autobiography, *White House Years,* "I cannot say that I fully understand Sadat's insight then. Great men are so rare that they take some getting used to."

Sadat did not want to argue and haggle over minor details. Sadat's philosophy on finding a solution to a problem was, as he recalled in *In Search of Identity,* "Approaching a given problem, I do all in my power to provide a radical and final solution rather than a temporary one."

On December 11, 1973, Kissinger and Sadat met again. Sadat informed the U.S. secretary of state that he had been planning to attack Israel again to remove them completely from the Suez area. Kissinger then told Sadat that if he were to make such a move, the United States would have to get involved.

Domestic problems within Egypt were still a huge concern for Sadat. Now that he had executed the war against Israel to regain Egypt's lost land, he was ready to sort out how to handle Egypt internally. Even with all the problems, Egypt was in a state of exhilaration because of success in the October war.

On April 18, 1974, Sadat published the October Paper. The paper emphasized the need to get rid of illiteracy in Egypt by expanding the school system and making children stay in school. Huge efforts were going to be made to improve social benefits, housing, and employment. A plan would be mapped out to improve Cairo as a suitable city to attract foreign investors. Also, the rural areas would be modernized with new farming equipment. Sadat wanted to educate his people to become managers and professionals to help boost the dragging economy. He encouraged the Egyptian people to open their own businesses to create commerce.

President Nixon had scheduled a visit to Cairo in June 1974. Huge crowds lined the streets to see the American president. Egyptians felt honored to have such a guest. When Richard Nixon resigned from office in August 1974, his successor was Vice President Gerald Ford. Sadat felt he had lost a valued American friend.

Egypt experienced an extremely tumultuous year in 1975. Sadat opened his arms to tourist and foreign investors. He emptied prisons and encouraged some freedom of the press. Egypt's freedoms increased as the country headed toward democracy. Wrongly informed by his men, Sadat thought that the economy was booming when in fact many people were starving. Violence broke out on the streets. Huge crowds yelling their discontent marched through Cairo. Some crowds smashed commuter trains. Israeli discussed these events in *Man of Defiance*. People chanted vicious lines such as, "Oh hero of the crossing, where is our breakfast?" Sadat was deeply disturbed by these events.

Sadat had lost touch with reality and took the marches and

chants personally. Instead of trying to fix the real problem of food distribution, he treated the unrest as a campaign against him. He accused communists of inciting the masses to rebel. Organizing a group to hunt the communists down, he executed a massive crackdown. It became a witch-hunt with no resolve. Eventually he came to realize that he needed to do something about the economy.

Sadat wanted to make another bold military move that would help Egypt's economy. He needed more weapons and went on a campaign to find arms from other sources besides Russia. He visited Bulgaria, Romania, and China. In 1975, China provided Egypt with spare parts and engines. The Chinese were pleased to have a relationship with an Arab country. All countries in the Middle East rejected China in April 1956 when it became the People's Republic of China.

The peace talks between Egypt and Israel seemed to reach an impasse. With huge guns still pointed at each other, Sadat decided to make a daring move. He was going to open the Suez Canal. For every year the canal was closed, Egypt lost over 200 million much-needed dollars. He also wanted to clearly establish the towns of Port Said, Suez, and Ismailia on the east side of the canal to be Egyptian territory. The towns were being rebuilt, and all the Egyptians that had earlier evacuated now returned to their homes.

The Suez Canal was littered with massive amounts of debris. Egypt's navy did not have ships big enough to remove the debris. Sadat mentioned his intention of clearing the canal to Kissinger and also pointed out that the U.S. Navy had ships that were large enough to clear it. Sadat wrote about the conversation in his autobiography.

Kissinger said, "Am I to understand that you're asking for assistance?"

"Yes," Sadat said.

"Well, give me an hour," said Kissinger.

He called the White House and then informed Sadat that a

In 1975, President Gerald Ford (left) and Sadat (right) met with Israeli Prime Minister Yitzhak Rabin. After some difficult negotiations, Rabin agreed to pull back from the Suez Canal, and return the Abu Rudeis oil fields to Egypt.

U.S. ship would be in Port Said within two days.

After opening the Suez Canal, Sadat flew to Salzburg, Austria, to meet with the new U.S. president, Gerald Ford. The purpose was to continue negotiations with Israel for the western section of the Sinai Peninsula, including the Abu Rudeis oil fields. Israel resisted the idea but eventually agreed to pull back 35 miles from the eastern bank of the Suez Canal and return the oil fields. Egypt agreed to let Israel have access to the Red Sea.

During the negotiations, Yitzhak Rabin, the new prime minister of Israel, was very difficult. Ford recalls in his autobiography, "He fought over every kilometer. . . . I recognized that the Israelis had a fundamental reluctance about giving up territory . . . but he didn't seem to understand that only by giving do you get something in return."

Peace was still on the agenda for the various negotiations between Egypt and Israel. However, at the signing of the second agreement, the Egyptian representative refused to shake hands with an Israeli. Peace was still very far off in the future.

Some Arab nations were disgusted by the agreements Sadat was establishing with Israel. On September 15, 1975, a gang of Palestinians headed by an Iraqi Arab attacked the Egyptian Embassy in Madrid, Spain. The ambassador and his two aides were taken hostage. The gang demanded that Egypt announce that the second disengagement agreement was a betrayal to the Arab cause. They wanted all negotiations to end immediately. Several Arab ambassadors had to get involved to gain the release of the hostages.

Jehan and Anwar Sadat visited the United States in 1975 so Sadat could address a joint session of the U.S. Congress.

7

Journey
of Peace

B ecause of the disturbances in 1975, Sadat decided to focus on
Egypt's economy. He went on a huge fund-raising campaign.
He approached the United States and was able to secure an
American aid program, totaling $1 billion. The money would be used
to create grants within Egypt and also supply food. He then visited
the Arab oil-rich countries and was able to obtain another $10 billion
in aid.

Even with all these efforts, Egyptians were getting frustrated and
were tired of promises from their leader with no immediate results.
Discontent continued to grow among the common citizens and
especially among students. They saw their future employment
possibilities looking bleak. To them, modernization produced no
relief to the current situation. The students began to look elsewhere
for solutions. The Muslim fundamentalists provided a solution,

which was to enforce Islamic ideals such as individual morality and social justice. The fundamentalists viewed modernization as a direct violation of Islamic principles. They wanted to restore Islam to the days of old and provide for the poor. People joined the Muslim fundamentalists in droves and saw them as a solution to the current economic state in Egypt.

In 1976 the Muslim fundamentalists group Repentance and Hijra kidnapped the minister of religious endowments in Egypt. The group saw this minister as a source of corruption in Egypt. As a condition for releasing the minister, the fundamentalists demanded that Sadat state in public that Egypt had not been ruled by Islamic principles and that in the future it would be. Unsure what to do, Sadat stalled for time. The fundamentalists did not have patience and executed the minister.

Through all the unrest, Sadat still held some popularity with the majority of citizens and was reelected in October 1976. Even so, he would have to give many speeches in 1976 to placate the masses. Sadat had promised the Egyptian people economic growth when there was barely enough food to eat. He had to explain that most of the money was going toward rebuilding the towns along the Suez Canal and importing new farm equipment. In the future, he said this would make the overall food production of Egypt more self-sufficient.

According to Raphael Israeli's biography, Sadat's speeches often included his "belief in Allah, in his Holy Book and his Messenger; a faith in the right, in justice, in peace and well-being; a faith in forgiveness, which drives people to build, not destroy, to unite, not to dismember; a faith that hoists the flag of serenity and love, not evil." He also sent out a warning to the Muslim fundamentalists that he would find those that teach false religion to Egyptian youth. Once he had found them, they would be announced to the public and then brought to court.

On the international front, Sadat was still concerned about Palestine. He had been unsuccessful in his earlier negotiations to reach an agreement with Israel regarding Palestine. He then

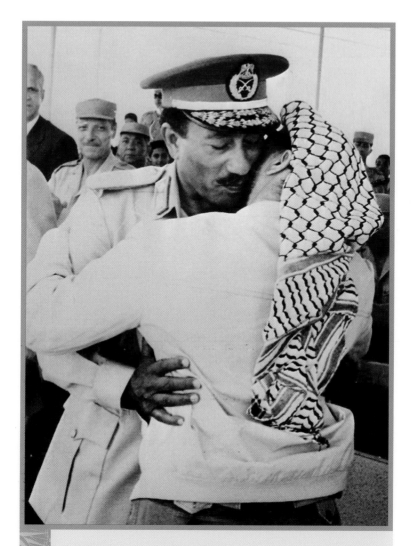

Sadat assured PLO leader Yasir Arafat that he would continue to support him in his quest for a Palestinian nation.

announced that 1976 would be the "Year of Palestine." He promised that he would campaign for a Palestinian national solution during his visits to Europe and the United States. Israeli wrote that Sadat then told the PLO leader Yasir Arafat, "Your problem is in good hands with Egypt, because it does not concern you only. My future, here in Egypt, hinges on that issue." However, Sadat was unable to keep his promise to Arafat. Instead the negotiations with Israel seem to have come to a standstill.

In January 1977, Egypt's internal problems escalated. The government faced major economic challenges and had to reduce government subsidies for basic food items such as flour, rice, oil, and sugar. Because of this action, prices soared. Hundreds of rioters took to the streets, smashed windows, and set buses on fire. Many were killed or injured and over a thousand were arrested. The riots first started in Alexandria but then quickly spread to Cairo. Sadat then addressed the nation and told the people that the prices would be reduced. He also criticized those in charge of organizing such riots and blamed it on the communist influences still in Egypt.

After the riots stopped, Sadat became aware of his faltering popularity. The poor were disgruntled because of his expenditures on extravagant suits, palaces, and traveling to foreign countries while they starved. Thousands of people flooded the streets and screamed, "Nasser! Nasser! Down with Sadat!"

Groups organized and attacked Western symbols in Egypt, such as nightclubs and bars where Western businessmen gathered. They also vandalized American- and German-made cars. Sadat knew that the Muslim fundamentalists were behind these attacks and was shaken by these events and felt apathetic. He also started to feel disillusioned with the Israeli negotiations. Knowing something drastic had to be done, he went to the United States to meet the new president, Jimmy Carter. Sadat immediately liked Carter. He was impressed that Carter was a religious man and had also grown up as a farmer. Carter's honesty and candor inspired Sadat to trust him.

Prior to visiting Washington, D.C., Sadat had drawn up a peace strategy and submitted it to Carter. Sadat wrote in his autobiography that he then informed Carter, "The very heart of the Middle East question . . . lies with the Palestinian problem.

It is ironical that some voices today call on the Palestinians to recognize Israel. How could you call on people who have lost their land, their state, and their very human rights . . . to recognize Israel?"

Sadat's peace strategy included establishing a Palestinian State on the Gaza Strip and the West Bank of Jordan. Also, he believed that Israel should withdraw from land they conquered during the Six-Day War in 1967. In exchange, Israel would be recognized as a state and there would be peace along its borders. Sadat fervently wanted peace with Israel. He saw the importance of this step for progress to occur in the Middle East. Meanwhile in Israel, elections had taken place, and Menachem Begin had been appointed prime minister.

In September 1977, Sadat received a personal letter from President Carter delivered via messenger. The contents of the letter were never fully divulged, but Sadat did mention that Carter gave him an up-to-date evaluation of the situation with Israel.

This evaluation led Sadat to think deeply about Egypt's relationship with Israel. He began to see Israel's objectives and motives more clearly and understood why the Arab world rejected these. The enormous wall of suspicion came crashing down on Sadat. It was a wall of hate, fear, and misunderstanding. Neither side, Egypt nor Israel, would believe anything from the other as long as it went through someone else, such as the United States. Sadat looked at these new realizations and decided to approach the problem from a new angle.

Sadat recalled in his autobiography, "It was then that I drew . . . on the inner strength I had developed in Cell 54 . . . he who cannot change the very fabric of his thought will never be able to change reality, and will never, therefore, make any progress."

Sadat was curious about Israel's Prime Minister Begin. Sadat contacted his friend President Ceausescu of Romania. Ceausescu had met with Begin extensively. Sadat asked the Romanian president what he thought of Begin. Ceausescu

Menachem Begin was Israel's prime minister in 1977, and he welcomed Sadat when he visited Israel to address the Kenesset. The next year Begin and Sadat negotiated at the Camp David summit.

immediately replied that Begin was a strong leader and he shared Sadat's desire for peace.

Thrilled with this new information, Sadat began to formulate a new initiative. He carefully reviewed all the data and made a decision. *Man of Defiance* portrays the situation this way: "Why should he drift down a course charted by others, rather than launch his own initiative, which would attract international attention, stun statesmen and countries around the world, and give the Israelis such a jolt that they would be rid of their fears and suspicions forever?"

On November 9, 1977, Sadat announced to the people of Egypt that he was willing to go to the ends of the world, including to Israel, for peace. He said that he would stand before Israel's parliament, the Knesset, if it would achieve Egypt's objectives.

Egyptian government ministers, as well as PLO leader Yasir Arafat, listened to the speech. They thought Sadat had made a mistake and had told a joke. Once everyone realized he was not joking, there was an air of disbelief. Some ministers and Arab leaders violently opposed such a trip, but Sadat stood firm. It was the last day Sadat was to see Yasir Arafat because he felt deeply betrayed by Sadat's objectives.

Visiting Israel meant acknowledging it as a country. No Arab leader had ever agreed to speak directly to Israel and now Sadat was opening the door to direct negotiations. He was trying to establish a permanent peace agreement, thus acknowleding that Israel was here to stay.

The contents of Sadat's speech spread to Israel and within a few days he received an official invitation from Begin to come to Israel. Deborah Rosen wrote in her book, *Anwar el-Sadat*, that Begin stated Sadat would be welcomed with, "all the hospitality, which both the Egyptian and Israeli peoples have inherited from our common father, Abraham."

On November 19, 1977, Sadat's "journey of peace" began. His plane taxied down the runway of Abu Suwayr airfield and took off toward Israel. Less than 40 minutes later at 8:00 P.M., Sadat's plane landed at Ben Gurion Airport in Tel Aviv. As Sadat walked down the steps of the plane, he saw a long receiving line waiting to welcome him. International television cameras were there to record the historic event. Prime Minister Begin energetically walked toward Sadat and firmly shook his hand.

Then the two leaders stood side by side at attention while the Israeli band played the Egyptian and Israeli national anthems.

In the receiving line, Sadat shook hands with former prime ministers, Golda Meir and Yitzhak Rabin, along with Foreign Minister Abba Eban and General Ariel Sharon. Sadat was then driven to the Israeli section of Jerusalem. He saw Egypt's flag flying everywhere and along the streets were huge banners written in Arabic welcoming him to Israel. Lining the streets were Israelis of all ages cheering him and waving Egyptian and Israeli flags. Tears welled in his eyes when he realized he had been wrong about these people and was delighted that he had gone on his journey of peace.

The next day Sadat visited the Arab section of Jerusalem. He headed to one of the Muslim world's holiest places, the al-Aqsa Mosque, to say his prayers. Later he would learn that while he was at the mosque, one of his daughters gave birth to a girl.

In the afternoon, he went to the Knesset to deliver his long awaited speech. The room was hushed and filled with television cameras. A feeling of tension was in the air along with excited energy as Sadat walked up to the speaker's platform.

Sadat's voice was commanding and he spoke frankly and with fervor. He told the Knesset that he recognized the fact that Arabs had rejected Israel, denied its existence, and refused to negotiate directly. He assured them that this was going to change. Egypt was willing to live in peace with Israel if justice was finally given to Palestinians and Arab territories. He reprimanded the Israelis for establishing a country of their own in a land that was not theirs to take and then denying a country to the Palestinians when the land was rightfully theirs.

Sadat likened his journey to Jerusalem to the story of Abraham sacrificing his son. He put himself in a dangerous and possibly life-threatening situation but through personal choice and spiritual strength, he was able to carry through with conviction. He informed them that only through personal strength and choice could peace be attained. He demanded that Israel withdraw from territories occupied since the Six-Day War in 1967. In return, Israel could be assured peace on its borders and friendly relations with its neighbors. He concluded his speech with, "So we agree, Salam Aleikum—peace be upon you."

After his speech, members of the Knesset clapped enthusiastically, and Israeli soldiers saluted him as a man of honor. Israeli leaders knew Sadat was a very unusual Arab leader and now the time was ripe to work out a peace initiative. Sadat viewed his visit to Israel as a sacred mission. Because of this, he gave his full attention to each talk and concentrated on each meeting. By the time he arrived at his hotel room, he was completely exhausted.

President Jimmy Carter (center) welcomed Sadat and Begin to the presidential retreat, Camp David, in September 1978.

8

Camp David

Five million people in Cairo arrived to welcome Sadat back from Israel. They cheered, shouted "hero of peace," and applauded him as he drove down the street. Sadat was overjoyed by the enthusiastic response. It was much more than he had ever expected. New slogans of "civilized road to peace" and "no more widows and orphans" became the norm. Newspaper articles praised Sadat's new peace initiative.

Sadat had made two decisions after his visit to Israel. The first decision was that there would be no more war between Egypt and Israel and the second was that Egypt would negotiate with Israel on how to increase security between the two countries. He presented these decisions before the People's Assembly and briefed them on what had occurred during his visit to Israel. The assembly thoroughly endorsed Sadat's proposal, and only 3 out of 360 members disagreed.

Sadat said in his autobiography that his major goal was "to put an end to the crisis in the Middle East by solving the Palestinian problem and effecting a withdrawal from the Arab land occupied in 1967."

Egypt's enthusiasm did not spill over into other Arab countries. Syria declared November 19, the day Sadat visited Israel, as a national day of mourning. Libya refused to have any more trade relations with Egypt and Saudi Arabia felt that Sadat had gone against agreements made by Arab countries.

Even though Sadat had accomplished a major milestone by visiting Israel, discussions between the two countries bogged down. Later, a meeting was called for Sadat and Begin to negotiate the withdrawal of Israeli troops on the West Bank of the Suez Canal. Begin made it clear that Israel had no intention of withdrawing. Frustrated, Sadat ended the meeting and called Begin an "obstacle to peace." There was still no solution in sight on how to handle the problems in Palestine.

Sadat began to feel isolated. Israel was not cooperating in withdrawing Israeli troops and other Arab nations were slighting Sadat for his relationship with Israel. Afraid that the relationship between Egypt and Israel may completely break down, President Carter stepped in. He invited Sadat and Begin to come to the United States for a summit meeting. The meeting was to take place at Camp David, the presidential retreat about 70 miles outside of Washington, D.C. Both leaders agreed, and on September 5, 1978, the meetings at Camp David began.

President Carter had gone out of his way to keep the atmosphere casual. The relaxed atmosphere at Camp David helped to lessen the animosity between Sadat and Begin. Carter allowed time for the two leaders to take walks, play tennis, and watch movies. Begin had brought his wife, Aliza, with him, but Sadat's wife, Jehan, had to stay in Paris because of a sick grandchild.

On the first two days, Carter met with each leader alone. Sadat handed Carter the Egyptian plan made in Cairo. Carter seemed surprised by the demands. Then Sadat confided the modifications he was willing to make. He pleaded with Carter not to tell Begin what those modifications were as it would make it hard to negotiate with the Israeli leader.

When the three men finally met, Sadat told Begin his proposal. Begin's face turned red and he could barely contain his anger. Biographer Peter G. Bourne wrote that Carter then said to the Israeli leader, "If you would just accept and sign the Egyptian proposal as written, it would save us all a lot of time." All three men broke out in laughter. The atmosphere seemed to become more warm and friendly to the point that Begin thanked Sadat for all the hard work he had put into the Egyptian proposal.

Over the next couple of days, Carter painstakingly defined the differences and points of agreement between Sadat and Begin. Sadat was pushing for the return of Sinai to Egypt and an agreement regarding Palestinians and the West Bank. He soon learned that Begin was willing to negotiate the return of Sinai, but fully intended on adding the West Bank to the country of Israel. According to Bourne's book, *Jimmy Carter*, Sadat confronted Begin and angrily said, "Security, yes. Land, no!"

Carter maneuvered the negotiations away from the Palestinian issue. Instead the talks focused on Sinai. But even then there was a deadlock between Sadat and Begin. Sadat ordered his men to pack their bags, as they would be leaving in the morning. Carter appeared at the door of Sadat's cabin late that night. He sat and talked with the Egyptian leader until after midnight. By the time they were through, Sadat had decided to stay. Even so, the atmosphere at Camp David seemed filled with despair and hopeless of ever achieving a resolution.

Sadat gave a list of issues that he refused to compromise on.

Carter had planned the summit talks to involve some casual meetings between the three leaders so that they could exchange ideas about the effects of war on the morale of a nation.

Beyond these issues, he agreed to have Carter's aides start to draw up a proposal. Carter presented a proposal addressing 50 different issues.

On the sixth day of the Camp David talks, Carter invited Sadat and Begin to visit the nearby Gettysburg Battlefields. The battlefields were a subtle reminder of agreements being settled by war and not negotiations.

Because of Israel's long-standing relationship with the United States, Carter went over the new proposal line by line with Begin without Sadat's attendance. Begin squabbled over the wording of some of the points. He especially did not like U.N. Resolution 242, which stated that Israel would not be allowed to get land by war. Carter began to lose patience with

Begin and started to doubt his desires for peace. Carter was later reassured that this was not the case. A new draft of the proposal was made and given to Sadat and Begin. Sadat's men studied the document for 24 hours. Then Carter had another agreement drawn up on how Israel was going to withdraw from Sinai.

On the evening of the eighth day, Carter was having dinner with Begin. The Israeli leader again brought up Resolution 242. He informed the U.S. president that he had already prepared a press release. The release thanked the United States for inviting Egypt and Israel to Camp David, but Israel could not sign Carter's proposal. Carter was furious at Begin, which led to a heated argument. However, Carter was not going to give up.

The next day Carter worked with Sadat's most militant assistant, Osama el-Baz, and Begin's trusted attorney, General Barak, to create a new draft of the proposal. They worked on it for over 11 hours. Most of the sensitive issues were ironed out, but when the topic of removing Jewish settlements from Sinai came up, Barak said that only Begin could address that issue. Later that night, Carter went to Begin's cabin to thank him for allowing his staff to work on the proposal. Begin immediately replied that he would not sign anything that removed Jewish settlements.

On the 10th day, in the early morning, Carter and Sadat went for a walk. Carter recalled in his biography that Sadat said, "Since the visit to Gettysburg, he had come to appreciate how Carter, as a southerner, must understand the hardships of rebuilding the spirit of a nation after devastating military defeat."

Later that day, discussions continued regarding the newly made proposal. There was broad agreement between Sadat and Begin, except on the Jewish settlements in the Sinai. Neither side would budge. Sadat went back to his cabin and began to pack his bags. Carter arrived at Sadat's door and begged him to stay. He informed the Egyptian president that if he were to leave, their political and personal friendship would come to an end. Sadat told Carter that he did not feel that Begin had any intention of signing the agreement. Sadat had agreed with everything in the proposal but was not going to make sacrifices if Israel was to make none.

The next morning, the 12th day at Camp David, Sadat got another visit from Carter. He thanked Sadat for participating in the talks and promised to visit Egypt with his wife, Rosalynn. There was a sense of failure in the air as no agreements were in place. Later that day, Carter asked the Israeli delegation to meet with him. A long discussion ensued regarding the Jewish settlements. Finally, according to Jimmy Carter's biography, Begin said that in two weeks he would submit the following question to the Knesset, "If agreement is reached on all other Sinai issues, will the settlers be withdrawn?" This was the breakthrough on the Sinai problem.

After flying to Washington, D.C., Sadat, Carter, and Begin met in the East Room in the White House, on the 13th day at 10:15 P.M. All three men signed two documents: the Framework for Peace in the Middle East and the Framework for the Conclusion of the Peace Treaty Between Egypt and Israel. In front of cameras, the three men smiled and hugged each other.

Sadat and Begin were two completely different men. However, after spending 13 days in Camp David together, they began to also see their similarities. They were both strong leaders who loved their countries and wanted peace. Throughout the negotiations, they had to decide when to give and when to take, showing the world their statesmanship and wisdom.

When Sadat returned to Cairo, his people welcomed him like a hero. However, both men had to face criticism. Arabs said that Sadat had recognized Israel as a valid nation and

On March 26, 1979, Sadat, Carter, and Begin clasped hands after signing the peace treaty between Egypt and Israel.

did not make the country give up the West Bank or East Jerusalem. Israelis were concerned they would lose the valuable oil fields in the Sinai.

At the same time, in September 1978, the president of Iraq, Saddam Hussein, called the heads of Arab states together to meet in Baghdad. The purpose was to formulate a plan to stop a peace agreement between Egypt and Israel. Sadat was first offered $5 million from the Arab countries to reject the treaty signed at Camp David. You can't buy the will of Egypt was Sadat's reply.

The Arab headquarters was moved from Cairo to Tunis, Tunisia. The PLO started terrorist's acts against Egypt and Israel. They attempted to bomb the Egyptian embassies in Cyprus and Turkey, but their plots were discovered. Even though he was deeply hurt by Arab actions taken against him, Sadat continued the negotiations with Israel.

During the negotiations, Sadat and Begin were both awarded the Nobel Peace Prize because of their efforts to settle the Arab-Israeli conflict. The Nobel committee praised Sadat's visit to Jerusalem as unprecedented. It opened the door that had separated the two countries for years. Sadat did not attend the prize ceremony in Oslo, Norway. He did not feel that peace had been attained by his talks with Israel and did not like the fact that the prize was shared with Begin. Sadat felt that he started the peace initiative and Begin was just along for the ride. The $164,000 awarded to Sadat was given to his native village, Mit Abul-Kum.

In 1979, Saddam Hussein hosted the Baghdad Summit. During the summit, it was decided to remove Egypt from the Arab League because of its peace treaty with Israel.

In March 1979, Carter flew to Cairo and Jerusalem with proposals to further the points of the initial peace treaty. Carter flew between the two cities until a final agreement was hammered out. Then on March 26, Sadat, Begin, and Carter signed the final peace treaty on the White House lawn in a huge tent. War had finally ended between Egypt and Israel. Also, the treaty laid out how Israel would completely withdraw from former Egyptian territory within three years.

Sadat praised Carter at the signing ceremony. In *Man*

of Defiance, Sadat is quoted as saying, "Jimmy Carter single-handedly brought about the miracle of the Agreement . . . and had achieved the greatest feats of our generation." By November 1979, Egypt peacefully regained control of over half of the Sinai Peninsula.

In 1980 peace talks failed between Israel's President Yitzhak Navon (left) and Sadat on the Palestinian-West Bank issue.

9

Assassination

T he Palestinian-West Bank problem was still unresolved. Eager to show other Arab nations that he could solve the problem through peaceful means, Sadat again engaged in negotiations with Israel. After 10 rounds of talks and no answer forthcoming, Sadat suspended the talks on May 8, 1980.

Sadat felt alone in the Arab world after 17 Arab countries imposed economic sanctions against Egypt. They felt he was a traitor because he had betrayed the Arab cause by trying to establish peace with Israel. It was asserted that Sadat only thought of Egypt and did not care about the Palestinian issue. In addition, he had lost a good friend and ally when President Reagan succeeded President Carter in the 1980 U.S. presidential elections.

Frustrated, he turned his attention to the internal affairs of Egypt. He was now 61 years old and had served as Egypt's president for 11 years. Many of Egypt's problems were the same ones Sadat had faced when first elected president. One of the largest problems was population growth.

Birth control was taboo as men were the supreme rulers in a marriage and children represented the strength of the man. The population growth put huge strains on Cairo, Alexandra, and other cities throughout Egypt. The government had a difficult time providing necessities such as water, electricity, and transportation. In addition, because of limited farmland in Egypt, 80 percent of the food had to be imported. To make food affordable to the common citizen, the government had to pay for most of the cost.

Women's rights were virtually unknown when Sadat first took office. His wife, Jehan, was very active in establishing women's rights throughout Sadat's presidency. In the past, when an Egyptian man wanted to take on a second wife, he could do so without the consent of the first wife. Now the first wife must be consulted and if the husband marries the second wife without her consent, the first wife can sue for damages.

Also, in the past, a husband could divorce a wife without telling her. Unaware of her new status, the wife would continue living with her "husband." If she were to have children with her "husband," he would simply say I already divorced you so I will not support the children. This action became illegal because of Jehan.

Egypt did have two bright spots in the economy. It produced enough oil via the Abu Rudeis oil fields on the Sinai Peninsula to supply its own needs and also to sell on the international market. In 1981, Egypt expected to make $1 billion through oil sales alone. Also, the Suez Canal was fully functioning. In 1980, the canal generated $600 million in tolls and was projected to bring in $1 billion in 1981.

In 1979, Muslim fundamentalist leader Ayatollah Khomeini became the leader of Iran's revolution. His ideas spilled over into other Arab nations. The concept that strict

Muslim fundamentalist leader Ayatollah Khomeini is greeted by supporters in Iran.

Islamic laws should be enforced on citizens became popular and the solution to Egypt's economic problems. Mosque attendance was at its highest ever and reed prayer mats began to appear in the hallways of public buildings during prayer times.

Sadat was a devout Muslim, but he did not agree with Khomeini's radical laws. Instead, he offered a safe haven to the ousted Shah of Iran. Sadat felt empathy for the terminally ill man who had been rejected by other countries. He was heavily criticized for giving refuge to the shah by some Arab nations.

But the shah had been a faithful friend to Sadat in times of need. During the October 1973 War, the shah had provided much needed oil to Egypt. Because of this, Sadat felt he owed the exiled ruler his friendship. The shah eventually died in Cairo on July 27, 1980. Sadat ordered a state funeral for his friend. Muslim fundamentalists were extremely angered by Sadat's actions toward the shah. It was taken as a blatant insult toward Khomeini.

Sadat then announced that he planned to build a mosque, a church, and a synagogue on Mount Sinai in Egypt. Muslims, Christians, and Jews considered the mount a holy place. Christians and Jews believe that Moses received the Ten Commandments on Mount Sinai. Muslim fundamentalists groups were appalled at the thought of a mosque next to Christian and Jewish houses of prayer.

The Muslim fundamentalists started organizing groups, which demonstrated against Sadat's political policies. Banners were flown criticizing Egypt's relationship with Israel. Leaflets were distributed saying that peace with Israel was evil and urged devout Muslims to prepare for a *jihad,* a holy war, against Israel by getting rid of the corruption within Egypt. Sadat heard rumors of assassination plots against him.

Egypt's native Christians, called Coptic Christians, became agitated by the increasing Muslim presence. They did not want Muslim rules applied to them. Sadat tried to balance his favor toward Muslim and Coptic demands, but in June 1981 a riot broke out between the two groups. Houses were destroyed, people were killed, and three churches were set on fire. Police discovered arms and ammunition being stored by the Muslims and the Coptics.

Sadat became furious, and in September 1981 he abandoned his ideals of democracy and freedom. The police force was strengthened on college campuses. He then launched an investigation into antigovernment activities. Suspects were pulled out of bed in the middle of the night and dragged away.

Sadat also resorted to tapping civilian's phones and hiring spies. These were activities he had condemned years before. He no longer acknowledged the Coptic Pope and banished him to a monastery in the desert. He came down hard on both groups and jailed more than 1,600 people. He again blamed Communism and banished 1,000 soviet civilians from Egypt. Sadat then publicly announced that lack of discipline within Egypt had stopped. Never had he been more wrong.

Identifying the incorrect cause of unrest led to Sadat's demise. Several Muslim fundamentalists groups were forming in Egypt based on the Muslim Brotherhood. The Takfir Wal Hijra, which strongly approved of sacred terror, proved to be the most deadly.

Sadat was unable to accomplish his desired goals with Israel. He became withdrawn and felt isolated from the world. Jehan said in *Man of Defiance*, "Once he attained peace with Israel, he would seek peace for himself."

Jehan remembered many times when Sadat would come home, and his shoulders seemed bent from the weight of his huge responsibilities. He would sit quietly in a chair puffing his pipe and detach himself from his immediate surroundings.

Many times Sadat described the happiness he felt while he was alone in his village, Mit Abul-Kum, or on the shores of the Mediterranean, watching the waves break against the rocks. He told Jehan that he had felt extremely close to Allah while viewing nature and was amazed by Allah's beautiful creations. Sadat decided that once he was done with public office he would return to his beloved Mit Abul-Kum. He began building a house on his favorite spot, a place where he loved to meditate. The unadorned house looked over a tributary of the Nile River. Lush green fields and orchards with mango and orange trees surrounded the rest of the house.

In September 1981 the people close to Sadat began to notice a change in his personality. In the past, he had always been a charming, deliberate, and calm man. He now seemed to be on edge and angry. He also lost his concentration while speaking and would jump from topic to topic.

On the morning of October 6, 1981, the anniversary of the October 1973 War, Sadat told his vice president, Hosni Mubarak, that he was feeling tired. Mubarak urged the president not to attend the parade but rather stay at home and rest. Feeling it was his duty to attend, Sadat dressed in his new field marshal's uniform with a large green presidential sash and took his place next to Mubarak in the stands overlooking the parade.

Meanwhile, Khaled el-Islambuli, a member of the Takfir Wal Hijra, had arranged to replace the soldiers assigned to one of the trucks in the parade. Three other members of the Takfir Wal Hijra joined him. Grenades and guns were hidden in the truck. They also arranged that after they carried out their plan and Sadat was pronounced dead, a radio broadcast would be released stating that Egypt was at the beginning of an Islamic era now that it had been freed of Sadat's rule.

The parade started at noon. A little after 1:00 P.M., low flying planes passed overhead for the air display. Sadat looked up. The truck that carried the Takfir Wal Hijra men drove closer to where Sadat was standing. El-Islambuli put a pistol against the driver's head and ordered him to stop. He then leaped out and charged toward Sadat. The Egyptian president stood up smiling, thinking that el-Islambuli was going to salute him. Instead, the terrorist threw a grenade at the stands. The other three men fired rapidly into the crowd. Quickly guards apprehended the men and once the smoke cleared, President Anwar el-Sadat had been fatally wounded. He was immediately airlifted out and within a few minutes died while being transported to the hospital.

One of Sadat's daughters, Camellia, recalls in 1981, before she left for Boston, she went back to Mit Abul-Kum to say farewell to her father. Biographer Raymond Carroll said in *Anwar Sadat*, "Before she left, he embraced her and said: 'Who knows if I will ever see you again.' Two months later he was assassinated."

This gunman, wearing an Egyptian army uniform, fired his rifle into the parade viewing stands during the attack that killed Sadat.

Khaled el-Islambuli was arrested along with the other three men. After an investigation, many others were also arrested for participating in the assassination plot. One of the men arrested was Ayman al-Zawahiri, who would later become the cofounder of al-Qaeda headed by Osama bin

Laden. When el-Islambuli was questioned as to why he killed Sadat, he said that Sadat had made peace with the Jews and was a traitor who had betrayed the holy laws of the Koran.

When Begin was first told the news of Sadat's death, he refused to believe such a story. But once he realized it was true, he became despondent and thought back to the special moments he had spent with the great Egyptian leader. Many international leaders attended Sadat's funeral, including three American presidents—Richard Nixon, Gerald Ford, and Jimmy Carter. Britain's Prince Charles; the prime minister of Israel, Menachem Begin; the chancellor of Germany; and the president of France were also there. Only 3 of the 24 members of the Arab League sent representatives.

Sadat had mentioned several times in his life that he wanted to be laid to rest in his little village of Mit Abul-Kum. But, it was decided that Anwar el-Sadat should be buried in a public site near the capital. President Hosni Mubarak explained in *Anwar Sadat,* "He was a statesman, one of the greatest in the world. How could you put him in a very small place?"

Tears streamed down the faces of the onlookers as Sadat's coffin was lowered into the crypt. Mourners walked by to pay their final respects and read the words on the tombstone:

> In the name of Allah, All Merciful:
> So not consider those killed for
> the sake of Allah as dead but alive
> with the Almighty.
> President Believer Mohammed Anwar Sadat
> Died on October 6, 1981.
> Hero of war and peace.
> He lived for the sake of peace and
> he was martyred for the sake of his principles.

In other Arab countries celebrations were in progress. Syria had radios blaring that Sadat, the Arab traitor, was now dead and also proclaimed it a victory to the Arab world. In some Arab countries, streets were filled with people chanting praises and dancing to celebrate his death. The PLO announced Sadat's death was a long awaited execution.

Anwar Sadat will be remembered for his commitment to peace and to the people of Egypt.

10

Sadat's Legacy

A nwar Sadat was raised in poverty, rose above the average man, and shone as a bright beacon in the Arab world. His desire for peace with Israel shook the Arab community to the core of its belief that Israel was to be destroyed. Sadat's ability to get rid of his own negative ideas that had been perpetrated since the beginning of the Jewish state was unique to him. Breaking out of the norm and looking beyond prejudices and hatred, he jolted Arab nations to try to find another solution for peace besides war and annihilation.

In his autobiography, Sadat recalled his address to the Knesset while visiting Jerusalem. He said, "For the sake of our people and for the sake of civilization . . . we have to defend man everywhere against rule by the force of arms so that we may endow the rule of humanity with . . . the values and principles that further the sublime position of mankind."

Two hours after the death of Sadat was announced, the Egyptian cabinet held an emergency meeting. Hosni Mubarak was named as the leader of the armed forces and as prime minister. He was also nominated for the presidency. On October 14, 1981, Hosni Mubarak was sworn in as Egypt's new leader.

The United States was concerned the new leader would shun America like Nasser and then realign with Russia. On November 8, 1981, Mubarak addressed the Egyptian people for the first time. He stated that Egypt would still honor previous peace treaties made with Israel. He also said that he would deal with the United States and Russia as equals. There would be no favoritism. Egypt's economy was going to be the first issue he addressed in his presidency.

However, Sadat left Mubarak a very perplexing problem. How was Egypt to end the isolation with the Arab world without also upsetting the ongoing relationship with Israel?

In 1982, Mubarak announced that the peace policy started by Sadat would not be changed. He informed the public that it took them many years to establish it and he didn't intend to throw it out. That year, Israel completely withdrew from the Sinai Peninsula, thereby fulfilling one of their promises in the peace treaty made with Sadat.

On the other hand, Mubarak also started to slowly "court" the other Arab countries by visiting Saudi Arabia and arranging a meeting with Yasir Arafat, the leader of the PLO. Jordan also expressed its desire to resume diplomatic ties. Israel was alarmed by these actions but did not cut ties with Egypt.

In 1985, Saddam Hussein argued with the Arab League that Egypt should be let back in. According to Hussein's biographers, Efraim Karsh and Inari Rauts, he stated, "Arab solidarity would never be the same without Egypt. It is simply too large and important to be left outside the Arab camp. Besides, Mubarak was not Sadat."

Mubarak was not as controversial as Sadat, but he still had enemies within the Muslim fundamentalists groups because of his ties to the United States and Israel. Throughout his presidency, he allowed and encouraged the Muslim Brotherhood to have members run for office in the Parliament. But time and again, plots by the Muslim Brotherhood to overthrow the government were discovered. On July 29, 2001, the Egyptian government arrested and brought charges against the Muslim Brotherhood, which was planning yet another coup against the government.

Mubarak has held to the peace promises made to Israel by Sadat. He has not engaged in war against the Jewish state and has continued peace negotiations with Israel.

It is as if the words in Sadat's autobiography still ring loud and clear, "It is not my battle alone. Nor is it the battle of the leadership of Israel alone. It is the battle of all and every citizen in all territories, whose right it is to live in peace. It is the commitment of conscience and responsibility in the hearts of millions."

1918	Anwar Sadat born on December 25 in the small village of Mit Abul-Kum.
1925	Sadat's family moves to Cairo.
1938	Sadat graduates from the Royal Military Academy and is stationed in Manqabad where he first met Nasser.
1939	Sadat forms the Free Officers' Organization.
1940	Marries Ekbal Madi.
1941	Arrested for relationship with Aziz al-Masri; released for lack of evidence. Stages an unsuccessful revolution.
1942-1944	Arrested and jailed for anti-British activities. He is held in the Alien's Jail and different detention centers.
1944	Escapes from jail and lives as a fugitive.
May 7, 1945	The Germans surrender and the British lift martial laws in Egypt.
January 1946-1948	Arrested and jailed for being a conspirator in Amin Osman's assassination. Sadat spends two years in Cell 54.
May 29, 1949	Marries Jehan Safwat.
January 15, 1950	Becomes a captain in the Egyptian army.
July 1952	Nasser and his supporters stage a military coup and overthrow and exile King Farouk.
1954	Britain signs the Evacuation Agreement.
1955	First arms deal struck with between Egypt and Russia.
1956	Nasser is elected president and claims the Suez Canal for Egypt.
1964	The PLO is formed.
June 5, 1967	The Six-Day War with Israel begins. Israel destroys Egypt's air force and takes over the Sinai Peninsula and Gaza Strip.
1968	Egypt starts the War of Attrition against Israel.
1969	Sadat appointed vice president.
1970	Nasser dies. Sadat is elected the president of Egypt.
1971	Announced as the "Year of Decision." Sadat contacts the Russians for weapons but receives none.
October 6, 1973	Sadat launches a war against Israel after receiving weapons from Russia.

1974	Kissinger starts "shuttle diplomacy" and finalizes a disengagement agreement.
June 5, 1975	Sadat reopens the Suez Canal.
1977	Jimmy Carter becomes U.S. president, and Menachem Begin becomes Israel's prime minister. Sadat visits Jerusalem.
1978	Peace talks are held at Camp David. Sadat and Begin are awarded the Nobel Peace Prize.
1979	Sadat and Begin sign peace treaty that ends war between Egypt and Israel.
October 6, 1981	Sadat is assassinated while watching a military parade celebrating the anniversary of the October 1973 war.

Rosen, Deborah Nodler. *Anwar el-Sadat: A Man of Peace.* Danbury, C.T.: Children's Press, 1986.

Carroll, Raymond. *Anwar Sadat.* New York: Franklin Watts, 1982.

Sullivan, George. *Sadat: The Man Who Changed Mid-East History.* New York: Walker and Company, 1981.

El-Sadat, Anwar. *In Search of Identity an Autobiography.* New York: Harper and Row, 1977.

Israeli, Raphael. *Man of Defiance A Political Biography of Anwar Sadat.* New York: Barnes and Noble Books, 1985.

Hirst, David and Beeson, Irene. *Sadat.* New York: Faber and Faber, 1981.

PICTURE CREDITS

ABOUT THE AUTHOR

SARA LOUISE KRAS has had several nonfiction books published in the educational field. She has worked in education for 15 years and has traveled extensively throughout the world. After completing an educational project in Zimbabwe, Africa, she now lives in Glendale, California.

ARTHUR M. SCHLESINGER, jr. is the leading American historian of our time. He won the Pulitzer Prize for his book *The Age of Jackson* (1945) and again for a chronicle of the Kennedy Administration, *A Thousand Days* (1965), which also won the National Book Award. Professor Schlesinger is the Albert Schweitzer Professor of the Humanities at the City University of New York and has been involved in several other Chelsea House projects, including the series REVOLUTIONARY WAR LEADERS, COLONIAL LEADERS, and YOUR GOVERNMENT.